MW01670549

NOTICE TO THE READER

Behindthechair.com and the haircolorists quoted in this book do not warrant or guarantee any of the products described herein or perform any independent analysis in connection with any of the product information contained herein. The parties do not assume, and expressly disclaim any obligation to obtain and include information other than provided by the manufacturer.

The reader is expressly warned to consider and adopt all safety precautions that might be indicated by the activities herein and to avoid all potential hazards. By following the instructions contained herein, the reader willingly assumes all risks in connection with such instructions.

Behindthechair.com and the haircolorists quoted in this book make no representation of warranties of any kind, including but not limited to, the warranties of fitness for a particular purpose or merchantability, nor are any such representations implied with respect to the material set forth herein, and the publisher shall not be liable for any special, consequential, or exemplary damages resulting, in whole or part, from the readers' use of, or reliance upon, this material.

All rights reserved behindthechair.com 2010. The text of this publication, or any part thereof, may not be reproduced or transmitted in any form or by any means, electronic or mechanical, including photocopying, recording, storage in an information retrieval system or otherwise, without prior permission of the publisher.

---

check out our other books!

$49.95

$19.95

to order:

behindthechair.com/shop

1-800-760-3010 x10

introduction:

Chocolate cake is chocolate cake, yet there are thousands of recipes for the sinful treat. Some people use only Belgian chocolate, some add peppermint chips, others swear by Tahitian vanilla. Their recipes are fine-tuned and finessed over time until the cake comes out perfect every time, with the baker's distinctive flair.

The same is true for haircolor. How many "recipes" are there for buttery blondes, cool brunettes and fiery redheads? Every color pro has his or her favorite formulas—developed over years of trial and error—the formulas that never fail, that always produce the color that builds a business and a reputation.

What if you could peek inside the formula files of the world's most famous colorists? Imagine discovering the precise "code" for Kim Vo's "Malibu Blonde" or Jason Backe's "Anne Hathaway Brunette"? How about learning exactly how John Simpson creates his signature "Vintage Red" or how Sahag Workshop's Doug MacIntosh calms a brassy blonde?

Now the world's top color pros have graciously thrown open their "recipe boxes" to share their favorite all-time formulas for creating stunning blondes, brunettes and redheads. In "Formulas That Saved Your Life," they also reveal their go-to corrective strategies for everything from hot roots to bland browns. They even kick up their heels and have a little fun when they unleash their favorite avant garde formulas!

So dig in! Feel free to serve up these formulas for your own clients…or use them as launching points for creating your own, custom "recipes." Remember, haircolor is a science and an art—master both and you'll delight your clients every single time!

Mary Rector-Gable
Founder & Creative Director of behindthechair.com
mary@behindthechair.com

behindthechair.com Publishing

© 2010 behindthechair.com

Edited by Jackie Summers
Compiled by behindthechair.com
Cover Image: René Antonio
Scruples

contents

pages

Single Process Blondes 3
Multi Process Blondes 13
Single Process Brunettes 45
Multi Process Brunettes 57
Reds 85
Formulas that "Saved your Life" 113
Avant Garde or Fun Formulas 135
Who's Inside? 160

single process blondes

1 Warm Beige Blonde

Marie Robinson
Sally Hershberger Salon
New York, NY

Existing level: 6, 7 or 8
Target level: 9

Formula
Schwarzkopf Igora Royal 1-oz. 10-4 + 1-oz. 10-0 + 1-oz. 11-0 + 1-inch strip 0-11 + 3-oz. 40-volume Igora Royal Developer

2 Lavender Blonde

Sue Pemberton
Joico Vero K-PAK International Artistic Director
Las Vegas, NV

Existing Level: 9-10 (natural or pre-lightened)
Target Level: 9-10 (lavender tone)

Formula
Joico Vero K-PAK Color ¾-oz. Pearl Blonde Toner + ¼-oz. Violet Intensifier + 10-volume Veroxide Developer

3 Khaki Blonde

John Simpson
Goldwell North American Guest Artist
Lewis Salon
McDonald, PA

Existing Natural Level: 7
Target Level: 10

<u>Formula</u>
Goldwell Topchic 20 ml 12 BS Ultra Lite Blonde + 5 ml Violet Ash Neutra Lites + 50 ml 40-volume Topchic Lotion

4 Intense Violet Blonde

Sue Pemberton
Joico Vero K-PAK International Artistic Director
Las Vegas, NV

Existing Level: 9-10 (natural or pre-lightened)
Target Level: 7 (purple)

<u>Formula</u>
Joico Vero K-PAK Color ¾-oz. Pearl Blonde Toner + ¼-oz. 4FV (Wild Orchid) + 10-volume Veroxide Developer

5 Amber Blonde

John Simpson
Goldwell North American Guest Artist
Lewis Salon
McDonald, PA

Existing Level: 8
Target Level: 10

Formula
Goldwell Topchic 20 ml 12GN Ultra Lite Blondes + 5 ml 8KG + 50 ml 40-volume Topchic Lotion

6 The "Has It Been Colored?" Blonde

David R. Stanko
Redken Haircolor Consultant
New York, NY

Existing Level: 7
Target Level: 8-9

Formula
Redken Shimmer One 1 ½-oz 9NA + ½-oz 8V + 2-oz 20-volume Pro-Oxide Cream Developer.

7 Soft Blonde with Violet/Ash Undertones

Christopher and Sonya Dove
Wella Creative Directors
The Doves Salon,
Santa Monica, CA

Existing Natural Level: 5
Target Level: 9-10

<u>Formula</u>
Wella Koleston Perfect 1-oz 12/61 + 2-oz 40-volume Koleston Perfect Crème Developer.

Perform partial highlight application throughout the crown. Process 50-60 minutes.

8 Platinum Blonde

Anita Gutierrez
Clairol Professional Color Master and Educator
Backyard Day Spa
Long Beach, CA

Existing Natural Level: 6 or 7
Target Level: 10-11

<u>Formula</u>
Clairol Professional Premium Crème 1 ½-oz. 12A + ½-oz. 10N + 4-oz. 40-volume dedicated developer.

Process 45 minutes.

9 Steely Grey Over Blonde

Sue Pemberton
Joico Vero K-PAK International Artistic Director
Las Vegas, NV

Existing Level: 9-10 (natural or pre-lightened)
Target Level: 9-10

Formula
Joico Vero K-PAK Color 1-oz. Silver Blonde Toner + 1-oz. Silver Intensifier +10-volume Veroxide Developer

10 Soft Sandy Blonde

Lucie Doughty
John Paul Mitchell Systems Editorial Director
Los Angeles, CA

Natural Level: 6
Target Level: 8

Formula
Paul Mitchell the Color 1-oz. 7A + 1-oz 9P + 2-oz. 30-volume developer.

Apply roots to ends, process 35 minutes.

11

Peachy Blonde

Nelson Chan
Nelson J. Salon
Beverly Hills, CA

Natural Level: 7
Existing Level: 9-10
Target Level: 9-11

<u>Formula:</u>
Aveda Full Spectrum Deposit-Only Color Treatment 40g #9 + 2g Dark RO + 42g 20-volume Color Catalyst Crème Developer.

Process 20 minutes.

12

Gwyneth Paltrow Blonde

Nancy Braun
Christophe Salon, Beverly Hills, CA and
Roy Teeluck Salon, New York, NY

Natural Level: 7 or 8
Target Level: 10

<u>Formula</u>
L'Oreal Majiblonde ½ tube 901 + ½ tube 902 + 30- or 40-volume developer (depending on the starting level.)

Process 45 minutes.

Optional balayage highlights: L'Oreal Majimeche + 30-volume developer to frame the face.

13

Milk White Blonde

Christel Lundqvist
British Colour Technician of the Year
hob Salons
Great Britain

Natural Level: 5 or lighter
Target Level: 9-10

<u>Formula</u>
Wella Color Touch 9/16 + 10/0 + Emulsion 1.9% OR 9/16 +0/000 + Emulsion 1.9%, depending on desired tonal outcome.

Process 35 minutes.

14

Crème Brule Blonde

Maria Guasta
Rusk Creative Team Member

Natural Level: 8 with 30% grey
Target Level: 9

<u>Formula</u>
Rusk Deepshine Pure Pigments Conditioning Cream Color 30g 9.003nw + 15g 10.03nl + 67g of 20-volume Deepshine Shine Enhancing Cream Developer.

Apply formula midshaft to ends, process 15 minutes, apply to root area. Process 40 minutes.

15

Cool Taupe Blonde

Teri Dougherty
Wella Guest Artist
San Francisco, CA

Existing Level: 8-10
Target Level: 7-8

Formula
Wella Color Touch 3 parts 9/03 + 1 part 6/35 + equal parts 1.9% Emulsion.

Process 10-15 minutes.

16

Buttery Blonde

Nury Lopez
Rusk Creative Team

Natural Level: 5
Existing Level: 8
Target Level: 9-10

Formula
Rusk Deepshine Pure Pigments Super Lightener 10-oz. SLN + 2-oz. 40 volume peroxide.

Apply to regrowth and process for 25 minutes; apply to midshafts and ends for an additional 10 minutes.

multi process blondes

17

Malibu Blonde

Kim Vo
Kim Vo Salons
Las Vegas, NV and Beverly Hills, CA

Natural Level: 6-8
Existing Level: 8
Target Level: 8/ash

Formula 1
Schwarzkopf Igora Royal 1 tube 9.1 + ½ tube 8.3 + equal parts 15-volume Igora Royal Developer. Apply one-inch out from roots.

Formula 2
Redken Lift 5/15 Cream Highlifting System + 40-volume Pro-Oxide Cream Developer.

Apply in desired foil highlight pattern. Process 30 minutes

18

Sun-kissed Baby Blonde

Christopher John
Garren Salon
New York, NY

Existing Level: 7 or 8
Target Level: 9 baby blonde with a touch of sun-kissed warmth.

Formula
L'Oreal Majirel Blonde 900S + 901S + 40-volume developer. Process 35 minutes.

Optional highlights
L'Oreal Basic White + 20-volume developer, around face and subtly diminishing toward crown.

Color Rinse
L'Oreal Richesse, equal parts Clear and Gold.

Apply to towel-dried hair and process 12 minutes.

19

Pure Flora Blonde

Lucus Etcitty
Vidal Sassoon Academy Color Director
Santa Monica, CA

Natural Level: 8
Existing Level: 10, pale gold blonde
Target Level: 10, pale cool blonde

Formula 1
Wella Blondor Crème Bleach + 20-volume Koleston Perfect Crème Developer. Apply to regrowth, process 40 minutes.

Formula 2
Tone with Wella Koleston Perfect 1-oz. 10/0 + 1-oz. 10/16 + 4-oz. Pastel Developer.

Apply to regrowth, process 20 minutes, apply to midshafts and ends and process an additional 15 minutes.

20 *Multi-Tonal Blonde*

Gina Khan
Logics International Spokesperson
Gina Khan Salon
San Francisco and Walnut Creek, CA

Existing Level: 7-8
Target Level: 9 with subtle dimensions

Formula 1
Logics Color Crèmes Permanent Gelucent Color 10 N + 20-volume Color Generator. Apply ½-inch away from scalp, through to ends in order to break the base. Work quickly and apply color in fine sections. Apply the same formula to scalp area, using a tint bottle. Remove color after five minutes to eliminate the risk of unwanted warmth.

Formula 2
Logics Light Reactions Powder Lightener + 20-volume Color Generator. Beginning in the fringe area, apply highlights to dry hair. Combine fine and bold weave sections. Under the part line, place a few foils back-to-back. Place approx. 40-50 foils along the sides of the head, framing the face, top and back of head and a few in the nape area. Process at room temperature until hair appears pale yellow, then shampoo.

Formula 3
Logics Imprints Demi-Permanent Gelucent Color 1-oz. 10N Sheer + 1-oz. 10B Sheer + 1-oz. Clear + 5-volume Color Generator. Apply to towel dried hair, roots to ends. Process at room temperature for 5-7 minutes.

21 Nordic Blonde

Stuart Gavert
Gavert Atelier
Beverly Hills, CA

Natural Level: 6-8
Existing Level: 8/brassy blonde
Target Level: 8/pure blonde

Formula 1
Redken Color Fusion 1 ½-oz. 9AV + ½ oz 9AG plus 20-volume Pro-Oxide developer. Apply to regrowth and process 40 minutes.

Formula 2
Redken Shades EQ 1 ½-oz. Clear + ½-oz. 9V + 2 caps 8GN + equal parts SEQ Processing Lotion.

Isolate a few strategic strands around the front hairline and tone all remaining midlengths and ends for 10 minutes.

22

Champagne Blonde

Silas Tsang
NAHA Color Finalist
Blushes Hair & Day Spa
Ottawa, ON, Canada

Natural/Existing Level: 7
Target Level: 10

Formula 1
L'Oreal Platinium Plus + 20-volume developer

Formula 2
L'Oreal Majirel 10.31 + 20 volume developer

Prelighten all strands to Level 10 very light yellow with Formula 1. Process 20 minutes. Tone all strands with Formula 2. Process 10 minutes.

23

Ali Larter Honey Blonde

Tracey Cunningham
Redken Creative Color Consultant
Byron & Tracey Salon
Beverly Hills, CA

Existing Level: 7
Target Level: 8-9

Formula 1
Shades EQ 9B + SEQ Processing Solution. Apply to roots and pull through to ends.

Formula 2
Redken Up to 7 De-Dusted Lightener + 20-volume Pro-oxide Cream Developer.

Apply to hairline and top sections using a balayage technique. Process to desired level.

24 Sunny Lauren Conrad Balayage Blonde

Kaz Amor
Redken Creative Color Consultant
Warren Tricomi Salon
Los Angeles, CA

Existing Level: 6
Target Level: 7

Formula 1
Redken Blonde Icing Conditioning Cream Lightener + 40-volume Blonde Icing Conditioning Cream Developer. Apply highlights throughout the head using a balayage technique. Shampoo but do not condition the hair.

Formula 2
Shades EQ 2-oz 9GB + SEQ Processing Solution.

Apply roots to ends, process 20 minutes at room temperature.

25

"Kim Raver" Blonde

Jason Backe
Ted Gibson Salon
New York, NY

Natural Level: 6
Existing Level: 9-10/highlighted with regrowth
Target Level: 9-10 cool highlights/7 golden brown lowlights

Formula 1
Wella Koleston Perfect 12/0 + 40-volume Koleston Perfect Crème Developer

Formula 2
Wella Koleston Perfect 9/01 + 40-volume Koleston Perfect Crème Developer

Formula 3
Wella Koleston Perfect 7/73 + 40-volume Koleston Perfect Crème Developer

Perform full head highlights, starting at the nape. Work in a herringbone pattern, following the shape of the hairline, alternating two packets of Formula 2 and two back-to-back fine slices of Formula 3. On the sides of the head, place four diagonal packets that follow the shape of the hairline—two packets of Formula 1, one packet of Formula 2 and one packet of Formula 3. Switch to horizontal sections and alternate single packets of Formula 2, Formula 3, Formula 1 and Formula 3. Repeat to the parietal ridge. On the top of the head, return to the herringbone pattern; apply one packet of Formula 2, two packets of Formula 1 and two fine, back-to-back slices of Formula 3; then repeat. Place two packets of Formula 1, one packet of Formula 2 and a fine slice of Formula 3; repeat twice more. Process 20 minutes without heat.

Formula 4
Wella Koleston Perfect 9/16 + 40-volume Koleston Perfect Crème Developer. Apply to damp regrowth to soften the base color, process 3-5 minutes.

Formula 5
Sebastian Laminates Cellophanes Honey Blonde.

Apply to all damp hair, process 20 minutes, covered and under heat; then 5 additional minutes without heat.

26

Cream-sicle Blonde

James Edick
Arrojo Studio
New York, NY

Natural Level: 7
Target Level: 10 platinum blonde

<u>Formula 1</u>
Wella Blondor + 20-volume Koleston Perfect Crème Developer.

Apply midshaft to ends. When approximately ¾ of desired level of lift is achieved, apply to scalp area. Observe scalp closely as hair lifts and remove when desired level of lift is achieved (approximately 40 minutes total.)

<u>Formula 2</u>
Wella Color Touch 10/01 + 10/03 + 0/000 (equal parts) + 1.9% Emulsion.

Apply roots to ends, process 10 minutes.

27

Light With Great Grey Coverage

Beth Minardi
BTC Color Education Director
Minardi Salon
New York, NY

Existing level: 7 with 75% grey
Target level/result: 9 with excellent and even grey coverage.

Formula 1
Goldwell Topchic 9KG + 20-volume developer.

Apply to pigmented hair.

Formula 2
Goldwell Topchic 9KG + 9NN + 20-volume developer.

Apply to unpigmented/grey strands. Process at room temperature for 45 minutes.

28 *Dimensional Beach Blonde*

Lucie Doughty
John Paul Mitchell Systems Editorial Director
Los Angeles, CA

Existing Level: 8 with remaining highlights
Target Level: 8 pale blonde with dimension

Formula 1
Paul Mitchell PM Shines ½-oz. 9N (Sugar Cookies) +½-oz. 8N (Brown Sugar) + 1-oz. Processing Liquid.

Formula 2
Paul Mitchell Dual Purpose Lightener + 10-volume developer. Divide head into four sections: a horseshoe section on the top of the head; a horizontal section from ear to ear, below the occipital; a vertical center part connecting the horseshoe to the nape (creating 2 additional sections.) Apply Formula 1 to the nape area and overlay with foil. Beginning on one side of the middle section, slice, apply Formula 2. Overlay with foil. Leave out a finer slice section above previous section. Create another slice above natural section and apply Formula 1. Create another slice above previous section and apply Formula 1. Continue working through the horseshoe section, alternating between the two formulas. Repeat on opposite side of head. On front sides, begin with a diagonal section that mimics the natural hairline and weave the first few sections starting with Formula 2. Then recreate the slice pattern as in the back, this time evenly alternating each formula. Section the horseshoe with the natural fall of the hair. Work around the horseshoe and hand paint larger sections. Continue to alternate formulas. Work up towards the natural part. Decrease the size of the sections and place them closer together. Use less of Formula 1 and more of Formula 2. Process 35 minutes.

Formula 3
Paul Mitchell PM Shines 2-oz. Clear Shine + 1 shot Color Shot Purple Violet + 2-oz. Processing Liquid. Tone roots to ends.

29 Glamorous Multi-Tonal Blonde

Patrick McIvor
Matrix Artistic Color Director
Patrick McIvor Color Studios
PA

Existing Level: 7 dark blonde
Target Level: 8-9 medium/light blonde

Formula 1
Matrix V-Light De-Dusted Lightener + 10-volume SoLite Cream Developer. Highlight hair in a pleating pattern.

Formula 2
Matrix SOCOLOR 8MM + 20 volume SoLite Cream Developer. Apply to non-highlighted sections and process for 30 minutes.

Formula 3
Matrix Color Sync SPM (Sheer Pastel Mocha) + Color Sync Activator.

Glaze entire head and process for 5-15 minutes until desired tone is achieved.

30

Mother of Pearl Blonde

Dhaniel Doud
Redken Haircolor Consultant

Natural Level: 6
Target Level: 7-9, mix of warm and cool tones

Formula 1
Redken Color Fusion equal parts 7N + 20-volume Pro-Oxide

Formula 2
1-oz. Redken Color Fusion 10N + ½-oz. Hi-Fusion Yellow + 1 ½-oz. 30-volume Pro-Oxide
Create a small triangle using hair from each side of the natural parting. At the tip of this triangle, create two more triangles toward the parietal. In each side triangle, alternate Formulas 1 and 2 in diagonal weave sections, working from the widest point to the narrowest. Repeat in the center triangle, working from narrowest point to widest; or apply Formula 3 in this section.

Formula 3
1-oz. Redken Color Fusion 8Gv + ½-oz Hi-Fusion Chrome + 1 ½-oz. 30-volume Pro-Oxide

Apply to all non-foiled sections. Process 35-45 minutes; rinse base color first and rinse until water is clear. Then rinse each foil carefully, one section at a time.

31

Speed Weaving Blonde

Lisa Marie Garcia
Farouk Systems Show Department Director
Houston, TX

Natural Level: 6N at scalp area; 8N-10N on midshafts and ends
Target Level: 10 with a mix of beige and gold tones

Formula 1
Sunglitz Crème Lightener Beige + 30-volume Sunglitz Developer on new growth.

Formula 2
Sunglitz Crème Lightener Natural Blonde + 10-volume Sunglitz Developer on midshafts and ends.

Formula 3
Paint brightening toners in Beige and Gold on top of lightener to create dimensional highlights. Use Speed Weaving Cap to place color. Process 10 minutes under low heat, cool for an additional 5 minutes.

32

Lisa Blonde

Brian and Sandra Smith
Matrix Artistic Designers
Dalton, GA

Natural Level: 6
Existing Level: 5
Target Level: 9-10 dimensional blonde

Formula 1
Matrix V-Light De-Dusted Lightener + 40-volume SoLite Cream Developer

Formula 2
Matrix V-Light De-Dusted Lightener + 20-volume SoLite Cream Developer

Using four quadrant sectioning and 1/8-inch subsections, apply Formula 1 from ½-inch away from the scalp through to midlengths and ends. Process until hair has reached 2/3 of desired lift. Using the same sectioning, apply Formula 2 to scalp sections. Process until desired lift is attained.

Formula 3
Matrix Color Sync 1-oz. 10N + 1-oz. 10V + 2-oz. Color Sync Activator (ck)

Formula 4
Matrix Color Sync 1-oz. 8N + 1-oz. 10WN + 2-oz. Color Sync Activator (ck).

Working in a herringbone foil pattern on top of the head, alternate slices of Formula 3 and Formula 4. Continue alternating the formulas in diagonal sections through the sides and crown. Apply Formula 4 to all remaining hair. Process 10 minutes at room temperature.

33

Strawberries and Cream

René Antonio
Scruples Artistic Director

Natural Level: 6
Existing Level: 6 (new growth) with 75% pre-existing highlights
Target Result: Level 7 strawberry blonde with golden highlights

Formula 1
Scruples Illusionist Brilliant Creme Highlights 8AN (Sandstorm) + Scruples Pure Oxi 10-volume Creme Developer. Apply to new growth to break the base.

Formula 2
Scruples Illusionist Brilliant Creme Highlights 7N (Candlelight) + Scruples Illusionist Accelerator Powder + Scruples Pure Oxi 20-volume Creme Developer.

Formula 3
Scruples Illusionist Brilliant Creme Highlights 8N (Spotlight) + Scruples Illusionist Accelerator Powder + Scruples Pure Oxi 20-volume Creme Developer. Alternate Formulas 2 and 3 in weave highlight sections.

Formula 4
Scruples Blazing Low Lights 6GN + 7GR + Scruples Pure Oxi Demi-Permanent Clear Developer.

Apply to all remaining mid-lengths and ends. Process 30 minutes.

34

Light Dimensional Blonde

Ellie Coates
Arrojo Studio
New York, NY

Natural Level: 7
Target Level: 11-12 bright, dimensional, balanced blonde

Formula 1
Wella Koleston Perfect 12/0 + 40-volume Koleston Perfect Crème Developer

Formula 2
Wella Blondor + 10-volume Koleston Perfect Crème Developer

Formula 3
Wella Koleston Perfect 7/71 + 10-volume Koleston Perfect Crème Developer

Alternate Formulas 1 and 2 in a partial foil highlight using a herringbone pattern. Divide the section below the nape into three subsections and apply Formula 3 roots to ends. Process 35 minutes and carefully rinse each section individually.

35

Three-Shade Dimensional Blonde

James Edick
Arrojo Studio
New York, NY

Natural Level: 7
Existing Level: 9-10 over-bleached
Target Level: 10-11 multi-dimensional blonde

Formula 1
Wella Koleston Perfect 10/1 + 8/71 + equal parts 20-volume Koleston Perfect Crème Developer

Formula 2
Wella Koleston Perfect 12/1 + equal parts 40-volume Koleston Perfect Crème Developer

Formula 3
Wella Blondor Crème + 40-volume Koleston Perfect Crème Developer

Divide the head into three sections—front right, front left and back. Alternate each formula using a bricklay pattern in the back and angled sections on the top. Process 35 minutes and carefully rinse each section individually.

36

Platinum Blonde

Victoria Benham
Kemon Artistic Team Member
Brown & Deline Salon West
Ann Arbor, MI

Natural Level: 7
Existing Level: 9
Target Level: 10-11

Formula 1

Kemon Liding Life Ultra Paste Lightener 1 packet + 60 mls 10-volume Uni Oxy Developer. Apply to new growth, process 20 minutes or until Level 10 is attained and comb off excess. Apply to midshaft and ends if needed and process an additional 20 minutes or until Level 10 is attained.

Formula 2

Kemon Actyva Coloro 10 1-2 parts + 6-volume Actyva Developer. Apply to entire head to neutralize unwanted tones. Process and remove.

Formula 3

Kemon Actyva Coloro 10.11 3 parts + 10-volume Actyva Developer.

Apply toner to all strands and observe carefully to determine processing time. Remove when platinum shade is attained on new growth and ends.

37

Halo Blonde

Doug MacIntosh
Sahag Workshop
New York, NY

Existing Level: 6 or lighter, virgin or previously highlighted
Target Level: 9-10 with lighter crown-area highlights.

Formula 1
Equal parts Clairol Luminize Liquid Lightener Clear + Luminize Developer. Apply roots to ends and process 7-10 minutes to break the base of the natural level.

Formula 2
Clairol BW2 Powder Lightener + 10-volume developer. Apply to weave highlight sections around the crown area. Process to desired level of lift.

Formula 3
Redken Shades EQ 1½-oz. Clear + ½-oz. 09NB + 2-oz Processing Solution.

Apply roots to ends and process five minutes at the sink.

38

Dimensional Baby Blonde

Berry Bachen
TIGI Academy
New York, NY

Natural Level: 7-8
Target Level: 10

Formula 1
TIGI Colour True Light + 20-volume developer. Pre-lighten hair to pale yellow

Formula 2
Equal parts TIGI Colour Radiant Gloss 0/02 + 8/0 + 8.5 developer

Formula 3
TIGI Colour Radiant Gloss ½ 0/07 + ½ Colour Radiant Gloss 0/00 + 2-inches Colour Mix Master 0/7 + ½-inch Colour Mix Master 0/22 + 8.5 developer

Alternate Formulas 2 and 3 in zig-zag sections throughout the head. Process 30 minutes.

39

Facets Blonde

Linda Yodice & Scott Cole
Paul Mitchell Hair Color Artistic Directors
Scottsdale, AZ and Atlanta, GA

Natural Level: 6
Existing Level: 8-10 (previous highlights)
Target Level: 9 in tones of sand, topaz and amber

Formula 1
Paul Mitchell PM Shines 2-oz. 9NG (Sandstone) + 2-oz. Processing Solution

Formula 2
Paul Mitchell PM Shines 1-oz. 3NG (Topaz) + 1-oz. Processing Solution

Formula 3
Paul Mitchell PM Shines1-oz. 6NG (Amber) +1-oz. Processing Solution

Create a diamond shaped section at the top of the head and secure with a clip. On the sides, create a V-shaped section beginning at the front of the diamond and ending at the back of the diamond. The point of the section sits just above the ear. Secure with a clip. Again on the sides, create a wide V-shaped section that sits below the previous one and ends in front of and behind the ear. Secure with a clip. Apply Formula 1 to the front, perimeter back and top of the diamond sections. Apply Formula 2 to the last section above the ears. Apply Formula 3 to the middle V section on the sides. Process 20 minutes.

40

Warm Dark Blonde

Kyle White
Oscar Blandi Salon
New York City

Natural Level: 5
Existing Level: 7-8 brassy yellow/orange bands w/uneven color
Target Level: 8 rich, warm blonde

<u>Formula 1</u>
Miss Clairol 30D + 20-volume Clairoxide Liquid Developer. Apply to regrowth, process three minutes.

<u>Formula 2</u>
Clairol Basic White Powder Lightener + 30-volume developer

<u>Formula 3</u>
Clairol Second Nature 2-oz. 138 + 1-oz. 137 + 10-volume Clairol Professional Developer.

Perform full head highlight with Formula 2, placing chunkier, thicker pieces around the front hairline and regressing toward the back. Apply Formula 3 in medium-sized weaves between the highlights (Formula 2.) Process to pale yellow.

<u>Formula 4</u>
L'Oreal Diacolor Gelee 2½-oz. Medium Golden Blonde + ½-oz. Medium Blonde + 3-oz. developer.

Apply roots to ends, process five minutes.

41 Radiant Blonde

Susan Roberts Cooper
TIGI National Creative Technical Director

Natural Level: 6
Existing Level: 8 midlengths and ends w/golden undertones and 1 ½ inches of regrowth
Target Level: Dimensional, "street style" shaded blonde, radiating from Level 6 (dark sand) around the perimeter to Level 8 (soft sand) in the internal sections and Level 10 (vanilla and pale cream) on top surface layers.

Formula 1
TIGI Colour Creative 6/1 + 20-volume TIGI Colour Activator

Formula 2
TIGI Colour Creative 8/1 + 20-volume TIGI Colour Activator

Formula 3
TIGI Colour Ultra Lift 100+/77 + 40-volume TIGI Colour Activator

Formula 4 TIGI Colour Lights Icy + 20-volume TIGI Colour Activator

Create an offset teardrop shape which comes to a point over the right eye, incorporating the crown. Create a crescent shape at the occipital, directly under the teardrop. The perimeter forms the remaining section. Apply Formula 1 to the perimeter at the root and extend to midlengths and ends. Isolate the perimeter with TIGI Colour Meche Strips. Apply Formula 1 to the root area of the crescent section. Starting at the left of the shape, create a diagonal back slice section and apply Formula 2 to midlengths and ends. Isolate with a Colour Meche Strip. Take another slice at the same angle and apply Formula 1. Work throughout the section in this manner, alternating Formulas 1 and 2. In the teardrop section, apply Formula 1 to the root areas. Beginning at the point above the right eye, create a fine diagonal forward slice, apply Formula 3 to midlengths, leaving out the ends and blending with the root color. Apply Formula 4 to the ends. Isolate with a Colour Meche Strip. Take the next slice at the same angle and apply Formula 2 to midlengths and ends. Take the next slice and repeat the first application. Take the next slice and apply Formula 1 to midlengths and ends. Continue working through the teardrop, alternating formulas in this manner, until all hair is colored. Process 35 minutes without heat.

42 Medium Blonde, No Warmth

Beth Minardi
BTC Color Education Director
Minardi Salon
New York, NY

Existing level: 6
Target level: 7 cool, matte blonde

Formula 1
Wella Color Touch 7/1 + Emulsion 1.9%. Apply as lowlights.

Process at room temperature for 40 minutes.

Formula 2
Redken Shades EQ 1 ½-oz. Crystal Clear + ½-oz. 09NB + ¼-oz. 09G + SEQ Processing Solution.

Apply to all strands.

43

Vanilla-Honey Blonde

Michael Elving
Affinage National Artistic Education Manager
Las Vegas, NV

Natural Level: 6
Target Level: 10 soft vanilla-honey blonde with multi-dimensions

Formula 1
Affinage Ice Crème Lightener + 10-volume developer

Formula 2
Affinage 10.32 + 20-volume developer

Formula 3
Affinage Infiniti Satin 5 parts .000 + 1 part 9.23

Apply Formula 1 in a dimensional pattern throughout the crown area. Apply Formula 2 between foils. Process 45 minutes. Tone with Formula 3.

44

Iridescent Blonde

Adriana Balea
NAHA Winner
Francesca's Salon & Spa
Toronto, ON, Canada

Existing Level: 7-8 medium warm blonde
Target Result: Pale, iridescent blonde

Formula 1
Wella Blondor + 20-volume developer

Formula 2
Wella Koleston Perfect 12/89 + 40-volume developer

Formula 3
Wella Koleston Perfect 12/00 + 40-volume developer

Formula 4
Wella Color Touch 10/38 + Pastel Developer

Alternate Formulas 1, 2 and 3 in back-to-back horizontal slice sections from nape to crown and from temple to temple. Process 30-40 minutes, shampoo. Apply Formula 4 to tone all strands; process five minutes.

45

Expensive Blonde

Mia Liguori McHugh
Scruples International Haircolor Educator and Vice President of Creative
Lakeville, MN

Natural Level: 7
Existing Level: 8
Target Level: 9 rich blonde with amber and maple lowlights

Formula 1
Scruples Powder Blonde Lightening Powder + 20-volume Pure Oxi Crème Developer. Pre-lighten the hair with a virgin application technique. Process the cold shaft at room temperature for 20 minutes. Apply a fresh mixture to the scalp and process an additional 25 minutes.

Formula 2
Scruples High Definition 1 ¾-oz. 00 Clear + 1-oz. 8G + 1/8-oz. 4BV + 3¼-oz. Pure Oxi Pure Demi-Permanent Clear Developer. Apply to damp hair, process for seven minutes.

Formula 3
Scruples Blazing 1-oz. 8NA + 1-oz. 7GR + 2-oz. Pure Oxi Demi-Permanent Clear Developer

Formula 4
Scruples Blazing 2-oz 6GN + 2-oz. PURE Oxi Demi-Permanent Clear Developer.

Create accent panels on dry hair.

Apply Formula 3 to the front fringe and two outer panel sections. Apply Formula 4 to the center panel. Process 20 minutes.

46

Natural Blonde

Lisa Vann
Etherea Salon & Day Spa
Seattle, WA

Natural Level: 6
Target Level: 8

Formula 1
Aveda Shades of Enlightenment 40g Daybreak + 80ml 40-volume Color Catalyst

Formula 2
Aveda Shades of Enlightenment 20g Sunrise + 20g Sunset + 80ml 40-volume Color Catalyst

Formula 3
Aveda Shades of Enlightenment 10g Sunrise + 20ml 40-volume Color Catalyst

Apply Formula 1 to new growth. Create a large, star-shaped pattern on top of the head. Apply Formula 2 to all five "points" of the star, blending into Formula 1. Apply Formula 3 to remaining hair at the crown. Process 45 minutes.

single process brunettes

47 Favorite Brunette Formula

Clark Wood
Garren Salon
New York, NY

Natural Level: 4-6
Target Level: 5 chestnut brown

Formula
Miss Clairol 46D + 20-volume developer.

Apply only to regrowth. Process 30-45 minutes depending on amount of coverage required.

48 Caramel Delight

Kim Vo
Kim Vo Salons
Las Vegas, NV and Beverly Hills, CA

Natural Level: 4-6
Existing Level: 6
Target Level: 6 caramel

Formula
Schwarzkopf Igora Royal ½ tube 6.1 + ½ tube 7.1 + ½ Tube 7.0 + equal parts 20-volume developer

Apply to regrowth only, process 30 minutes.

49

Medium Ash Brown

Nelson Chan
Nelson J. Salon
Beverly Hills, CA

Natural Level: 5-7
Target Level: Level 5 rich, cool brunette

Formula
Aveda Full Spectrum Deposit-Only Color 40g #4 or #5 + 2g BG + 42g 20-volume developer

Processing Time: 20 Minutes

50

"Katie Holmes" Brunette

Nancy Braun
Christophe Salon, Beverly Hills, CA &
Roy Teeluck Salon, New York NY

Natural Level: 4/5
Target Level: 5

Formula
L'Oreal Richesse ½ tube 4.15 + ½ tube 5 + 9-volume developer. Process 20 minutes.

Optional balayage highlights
L'Oreal Platinium Plus+ 30-volume developer, concentrated around the face.

51 Chocolate Brown

John Simpson
Goldwell North American Guest Artist
Lewis Salon
McDonald, PA

Natural Level: 4-6
Target Level: 6 cool chocolate brown

Formula
Goldwell Topchic 40ml 10-volume + 25ml 5MB + 15ml 4V.

Process 35 minutes.

52 Caramel & Toffee

Sue Pemberton
Joico Vero K-PAK International Artistic Director
Las Vegas, NV

Natural Level: 6
Target Level: 6-7 caramel and toffee "lights" in a brunette base

Formula
Joico Vero Ultra Powder Lightener in Butterscotch, Caramel and/or Toffee + 10-, 20- or 30-volume developer (depending on depth of natural level.)

53 Rich Chocolate with Warm and Cool Accents

(as seen on Model Hilary Rhoda in the Elizabeth Arden campaign

Marie Robinson
Sally Hershberger Salon
New York, NY

Natural level: 4-7
Target level: 5-6

Formula
Goldwell Topchic 1-oz. 5N + ½-oz. 5A + ½-oz. 6NN + ½-oz. 5RB + 2 ½-oz. 20-volume developer

Foil fine panels of hair 1 ½-inches apart to add dimension to natural brunette shade. Process 30 minutes.

54 Keep The Red Out

Beth Minardi
BTC Color Education Director
Minardi Salon
New York, NY

Existing level: 4
Target level/Result: 4 soft brown with grey coverage and no red

Formula
Redken Shades EQ equal parts 06G + 08N + SEQ Processing Solution. Process with heat for 15 minutes; cool for 10 minutes.

55 Dark Brunette

Anita Gutierrez
Clairol Professional Color Master and Educator
Backyard Day Spa
Long Beach, CA

Natural Level: 3-4
Target Level: 4-5 rich, shiny brown

Formula
Clairol Professional Premium Crème 1 ½-oz. 4NN + ½-oz. 5GN + 2-oz. 20-volume dedicated developer

Process 30 minutes.

56 Rich Chocolate Brown

Lucie Doughty
John Paul Mitchell Systems Editorial Director
Los Angeles, CA

Natural Level: 5
Target Level: 4 deep, rich chocolate brown with balanced warm and cool tones

Formula
Paul Mitchell The Color ¼-oz 4VR + 1-oz. 3G + 1-oz. 4N + 2 ¼-oz. 20-volume developer.

Apply roots to ends, process 35 minutes.

57

Vintage Oak Brown

Christel Lundqvist
British Colour Technician of the Year
hob Salons
Great Britain

Natural Level: 5 or lighter
Target Level: 5

Formula
Wella Koleston Perfect 5/75 + 55/66 + 6% developer.

Process 30-40 minutes.

58

Stunning Brunette

Michael Elving
Affinage National Artistic Education Manager
Las Vegas, NV

Natural Level: 5
Target Level: 5/6 dimensional brunette

Formula
Affinage 2-oz. 5.036 + 1-oz 0.1 Green Intensives + 2-oz. 10-volume developer

Optional second formula for honey brown dimension:
Affinage 12.0s + 30-volume developer

59 *Khaki Tan*

John Simpson
Goldwell North American Guest Artist
Lewis Salon
McDonald, PA

Natural Level: 6-7
Target Level: 6-7 neutral (also makes a great lowlight)

<u>Formula</u>
Goldwell Topchic 40ml 20-volume + 30ml 7MB + 15ml 6BG.

Process 35 minutes.

60 *Favorite Brown Base Color*

Sue Pemberton
Joico Vero K-PAK International Artistic Director
Las Vegas, NV

Natural/Existing Level: 4-6
Target Level: 4 chocolate brown with auburn tone

<u>Formula</u>
Equal parts Joico Vero K-PAK Chrome RB4 + Activator.

Apply to all strands.

61 *Catherine Brunette*

David Adams
RedCHOCOLATE
Minneapolis, MN

Natural Level: 4
Target Level: 5

Formula
Aveda Full Spectrum Protective Crème Hair Color 4N + 10-volume Color Catalyst

Optional highlights
Aveda Enlightener Powder Lightener + 10-volume Color Catalyst

Process 30 minutes.

62 *Gray Coverage Brunette*

Teri Dougherty
Wella Guest Artist
San Francisco, CA

Natural Level: 5 with 50% grey
Target Level: 5

Formula
Wella Koleston Perfect 2-oz. 5/71 + 1-inch 0/66 + 2-oz. 10-volume developer

Note: for cooler results, add more of the 0/66 Violet Special Mix.
Process 30-40 minutes.

63 Medium 'Br-onde'

David R. Stanko
Redken Haircolor Consultant
New York, NY

Natural Level: 5 with up to 50% grey
Target Level: 6 medium "br-onde"—the perfect combination of brunette and blonde!

<u>Formula</u>
Redken Color Fusion 1 ½-oz. 6BGb + ½-oz. 7NN + 2-oz. 20-volume Pro-Oxide Cream Developer.

Apply to regrowth, then pull through during the last five minutes of processing. Total processing time: 40 minutes at room temperature.

64 Chocolate Brown Shade

Sue Pemberton
Joico Vero K-PAK International Artistic Director
Las Vegas, NV

Natural/Existing Level: 4-6
Target Level: 5 brown with slight red undertone

<u>Formula</u>
Joico Vero K-PAK Chrome ½ 4N + ½ 6RR + 10-volume developer.

65 *Cappuccino Brunette*

Silas Tsang
NAHA Color Finalist
Blushes Hair & Day Spa
Ottawa, ON, Canada

Natural Level: 7
Target Level: 5 creamy brunette

Formula
L'Oreal Luocolor ½ tube 5.12 + ½ tube Luocolor 5.3 + Luocolor 25-volume Developer.

Process 20 minutes.

multi process brunettes

66 Golden Safari

Joel Warren
Warren Tricomi Salon
New York, NY

Natural/Existing Level: 5
Target Level: 6-7 golden brown

Formula 1
L'Oreal Richesse 1 tube 8.30 Gold + 9-volume developer

Formula 2
L'Oreal Richesse 1 tube 5.3 Brown Sugar + 2.6-oz. Hi.Richesse 15-volume developer.

Part hair in a zig-zag from hairline to nape. From each side of the parting, apply Formula 1 to weave sections to create a zebra effect. Apply Formula 2 to all remaining strands between foiled sections.

67 Bronze Glow

Christopher and Sonya Dove
Wella Creative Directors
The Doves Salon
Santa Monica, CA

Natural/Existing Levels: 6 at the roots; 8 and brassy at the ends
Target Level: 6 rich, warm, velvety brunette

Formula 1
Wella Koleston Perfect equal parts 6/7 + 6/74 + 20-volume Koleston Perfect Crème Developer.

Apply to regrowth area.

Formula 2
Wella Koleston Perfect equal parts 6/7 + 6/74 + 30-volume Koleston Perfect Crème Developer.

Apply to midlengths and ends. Process 30 minutes.

68 Deep Wooden Mahogany

Berry Bachen
TIGI Academy
New York, NY

Natural Level: 5 or below
Target Level: 5

Formula 1
¾ TIGI Colour Creative 5/5 + ¼ TIGI Colour Creative 4/0 + 6-inches TIGI Colour MixMaster 0/77 (base color).

Formula 2
TIGI Colour Radiant Gloss 1/0. (lowlights)

69 Light Chocolate Fringe

Nury Lopez
Rusk Creative Team

Natural Level: 3
Existing Level: 4
Target Level: 6

Formula 1
Rusk Deepshine 1-oz. 7.8ch + 2-oz. 40-volume developer.

Formula 2
Rusk Deepshine 1 tube 5.8ch + 20-volume developer.

Create a zig-zag parting from the center of each brow, approximately 1-2 inches behind the hairline. Apply Formula 1 first to ends, then to scalp area of the fringe section. Apply Formula 2 to all remaining hair. Process 35 minutes.

70

Staurolite Brunette

Linda Yodice and Scott Cole
Paul Mitchell Hair Color Artistic Directors
Scottsdale, AZ and Atlanta, GA

Natural Level: 4
Existing Level: 4
Target Level: 5-6

Formula 1
Paul Mitchell The Color 2-oz. 4RB + 2-oz. 20-volume Cream Developer

Formula 2
Paul Mitchell The Color 1-oz. 5RB + 1-oz. 20-volume Cream Developer

Formula 3
Paul Mitchell The Color 1-oz. 6RB + 1-oz. 30-volume Cream Developer

Formula 4
Paul Mitchell The Color 1-oz. 7RB + 1-oz. 20-volume Cream Developer

Section 1: Create a rectangular section from the front hairline across the top, ending above the occipital bone on the opposite side. The width of the section is determined by the desired end result. Secure with a clip.

Section 2: Create a rectangular section on the opposite side from the hairline to the previous section. Secure with a clip.

Section 3: Create a final rectangular section opposite Section 2, ending above the occipital bone. This will create an 'X' pattern across the top of the head shape. Secure with a clip.

Apply Formula 1 to the perimeter back, sides and front.
Apply Formula 2 to Section 3.
Apply Formula 3 to Section 1.
Apply Formula 4 to Section 2.
Process 35 minutes.

71

"Lindsay Price" Brunette

Charles Baker Strahan
Rare Salon
New York, NY

Natural Level: 5
Target Level: 6 "sunlit" soft brown

Formula 1
Redken Double Fusion N + 20-volume Pro-Oxide Cream Developer.

Apply roots to ends or as foil highlights to desired areas. Process 35 minutes.

Formula 2
Redken Shades EQ 7GB + SEQ Processing Solution.

Glaze roots to ends.

72

Varied Hues of Brown

Ellie Coates
Arrojo Studio
New York, NY

Natural Level: 5
Target Level: 8-9 caramel highlights in a light brown base

Formula 1
Wella Koleston Perfect 12/11 + 40-volume Koleston Perfect Crème Developer

Formula 2
Wella Koleston Perfect 9/2 + 30-volume Koleston Perfect Crème Developer

Formula 3
Wella Koleston Perfect 7/73 + 20-volume Koleston Perfect Crème Developer

Place foil highlights throughout the hair, alternating the three formulas. Process 35 minutes.

73

Auburn Shades

Gina Khan
Logics International spokesperson
Gina Khan Salon
San Francisco and Walnut Creek, CA

Natural Level: 5
Target Level: 4 deep red brunette with subtle redwood shimmer

<u>Formula 1</u>
Logics Colorcremes Permanent Gelucent Color equal parts 4R + 6N (neutral) + 20-volume Color Generator. Beginning in the fringe area, apply to very fine foil weave sections. Place approximately 15-20 foils throughout the head.

<u>Formula 2</u>
Logics Imprints Demi-Permanent Gelucent Color 2-oz. 4N FULL + ½-oz. 4R FULL + 1-oz. 4G SHEER + equal parts 10-volume Color Generator.

Apply to all remaining hair. Process 15 minutes at room temperature.

74

Milk Chocolate

Doug MacIntosh
Sahag Workshop
New York, NY

Natural level: 4-6
Target level: 5-6 warm brunette

Formula 1
Wella Koleston Perfect 1 ¼-oz. 5 +¼-oz. 6/3 + 2-oz. 20-volume Koleston Perfect Crème Developer. Apply roots to ends, process 30 minutes.

Formula 2
Clairol Basic White Powder Lightener + 5-volume developer. Apply foil highlights throughout face and crown areas.

Formula 3
Redken Shades EQ 2-oz. 07G + ¼-oz. 06WG + 2 ¼-oz. SEQ Processing Solution. (For less warmth--Redken Shades EQ 06G + SEQ Processing Solution.)

Glaze all strands.

75

Rich Chocolate Brown

Francesco Fricioni
Oscar Blandi Salon
New York, NY

Natural Level: 1-6
Existing Level: 6-7 with 25% grey
Target Level: 6

Formula 1
Wella Color Touch 1 tube #60 + ¼ tube 677 + 1 ½-oz. 1.9% Emulsion + 1½-oz. 4.0 developer (ck)

Formula 2
Clairol Born Blonde Crème Hair Lightener 1 bottle + 1 ½-oz. 20-volume developer + 2 activators

Formula 3
L'Oreal Professionnel Diacolor Light Chestnut + 1.9% developer.

Apply Formula 1 to scalp area, process 30 minutes and shampoo. Blow dry and place highlights around the hairline and crown areas with Formula 2. Process 20 minutes, rinse and towel dry. Glaze all hair with Formula 3. Process five minutes.

76

Beached Brown Hair

Patrick McIvor
Matrix Artistic Color Director
Patrick McIvor Color Studios
PA

Natural Level: 6 light brown
Existing Level: 5 medium brown
Target Level: 7 multi-tonal, sexy, beach-y brown

Formula 1
Matrix SoColor UL-A + double 40-volume SoLite Cream Developer. Take random slices throughout the head, 1/8-inch to 1/4-inch at the base, and backcomb pushing half of the sliced section away. Place remaining hair in foil and apply highlighting formula from the edge of the backcombing to the ends. Process 20 minutes. Do not remove the foils.

Formula 2
Matrix Color Sync 8WM + Color Sync Activator.

Apply to all hair between foils and process 20 minutes more. Rinse between the foils, then remove the foils.

77 Teak Undertones

Kaz Amor
Redken Creative Color Consultant
Warren Tricomi Salon
Los Angeles, CA

Natural Level: 5 with 25% grey
Target Level: 6 rich brown with teak undertones

Formula 1
Redken Color Gels ¾-oz. 5NA + ¼-oz. 5NW + 1-oz. 20-volume Redken Color Gels Developer.

Apply to all strands and process.

Formula 2
Redken Shades EQ 07 MV + SEQ Processing Solution

Apply to all strands and process 20 minutes.

78 "Peggy" Brunette

Lisa Vann
Etherea Salon & Day Spa
Seattle, WA

Natural Level: 5 with 25% grey
Target Level: 5 with golden honey highlights

Formula 1
Aveda Full Spectrum Permanent 40g 5N + 4g Dark Blue/Violet Pure Tone + 4g Dark Yellow/Orange Pure Tone + 40ml 20-volume Color Catalyst

Formula 2
Aveda Enlightener + 1-oz. 20-volume Color Catalyst

Apply Formula 1 roots to ends. Place processing hair in stand-up pincurls. Trace each curl with Formula 2. Process 30 minutes.

79

Warm, Full-Bodied Brown

Tracey Cunningham
Redken Creative Color Consultant
Byron & Tracey Salon
Beverly Hills, CA

Natural Level: 4-5
Target Level: 6

<u>Formula 1</u>
Redken Color Fusion 5N + 5NW + 10- or 20-volume Pro-oxide Cream Developer, depending on desired amount of lift. Apply to all strands, process 35 minutes.

<u>Formula 2</u>
Redken Shades EQ 5MV + SEQ Processing Solution.

Apply to all strands, process 20 minutes.

80 Violet Topaz Brown

Dhaniel Doud
Redken Haircolor Consultant

Natural Level: 4-5
Target Level: Cool 5 green melting into violet

Formula 1
Redken Color Fusion 4Ag + 20-volume Pro-Oxide

Formula 2
Redken Color Fusion ½-oz. 4Ag + ½-oz. 6Ag + ½-oz. Hi-Fusion Green + 30-volume Pro-Oxide

Formula 3
Redken Color Fusion 1-oz. 6Mv + ½-oz. Hi-Fusion Violet + 30-volume Pro-Oxide

Formula 4
Redken Color Fusion 1-oz. 6Ag + ½-oz Hi-Fusion Green + 20-volume Pro-Oxide

Create a diamond section on the high point of the head and secure. Create a larger diamond around the first diamond, and a larger diamond surrounding that. Overall size of the three diamonds combined should start at the hairline and extend to the crown. The width should be no deeper than the parietal.

Apply Formula 1 to all strands outside of the diamond sections. Proceed to the outer tier diamond. Starting on any side, take a fine slice, place on top of foil and apply Formula 2 from scalp to ends. Continue to drop down fine sections until all sides of the diamond are complete. Cover with foil and secure. Move to the next diamond and repeat, using Formula 3. Complete all four sides. Repeat on the uppermost diamond, using Formula 4. Process 35 minutes.

81 Velvet Brown

Kazumi Morton
Eiji Salon
New York, NY

Natural Level: 4
Existing Level: 6, with brassy orange tone on midshafts and ends
Target Level: 5 rich brown

Formula 1
Redken Color Fusion 1-oz. 5MV + 1-oz 5GB + 2-oz. 20-volume Pro-Oxide

Formula 2
Redken Shades EQ 1-oz. 5MV + 1-oz. 6NB + 2-oz. Processing Solution

Apply Formula 1 to regrowth and Formula 2 to midshafts and ends. Process 30 minutes.

82 Deep, Rich Brown

Adriana Balea
NAHA Winner
Francesca's Salon & Spa
Toronto, ON, Canada

Natural Level: 6
Target Level: 5 deep brown

Formula 1
Wella Koleston Perfect 6/71 + 20-volume developer

Formula 2
Wella Koleston Perfect 4/75 + 20-volume developer

Formula 3
Wella Color Touch 6/77 + 6/71 + 1.9% developer

Create two large triangular panels off of the natural parting. Create two more triangular partings off of the original triangular sections and a final large triangle in the back of the head. Alternate Formulas 1 and 2 in back-to-back slices within each triangular section. Apply Formula 3 to all remaining strands. Process 30-40 minutes.

83 "Anne Hathaway" Multi-Tone Brunette

Jason Backe
Ted Gibson Salon
New York, NY

Natural Level: 5
Existing Level: 6 with lots of exposed warmth
Target Level: 5/6 (neutral/cool)

Formula 1
Wella Koleston Perfect ½ 5/1 + ½ 6/2 + 20-volume developer (apply to regrowth).

Formula 2
Wella Koleston Perfect ½ 7/1 + ½ 6/71 + 1.9% developer (apply to midshafts and ends)

Process Formula 1 and 2 for 35 minutes

Formula 3
Wella Blondor + 10-volume developer, placed in foil packets along and underneath a center parting.

Process 10-15 minutes.

Formula 4
Sebastian Cellophanes 1/3 Deep Brunette + 1/3 Pearl Blonde + 1/3 Clear.

Apply to damp hair and process 20 minutes.

84

Classic Brunette Highlights

Lucus Etcitty
Vidal Sassoon Academy Color Director
Santa Monica, CA

Natural Level: 4
Target Level: 6 caramel brown

Formula 1
Wella Koleston Perfect 9/1 + 40-volume developer

Formula 2
Wella Koleston Perfect 7/73 + 30-volume developer

Apply full head, classic weave highlights, alternating formulas, using fine weaves for a natural result. Process 30 minutes.

85

Camilla Brunette

David Adams
RedCHOCOLATE
Minneapolis, MN

Natural Level: 3
Target Level: 5

Formula 1
Aveda Full Spectrum Deep Crème Color 6Y/O + 20-volume Color Catalyst

Formula 2
Aveda Full Spectrum Deep Crème Color 10B/GR with 30-volume Color Catalyst

Formula 3
Aveda Full Spectrum Deep Crème Color 12Y/G with 40-volume Color Catalyst

Apply Formula 1 to new growth; alternate Formulas 2 and 3 on midshafts and ends. Process 20 minutes.

86 Jennifer Lopez Multi-Tone Brunette

Tracey Cunningham
Byron and Tracey Salon
Redken Creative Color Consultant
Beverly Hills, CA

Natural Level: 6
Target Level: 6-8 shiny brunette with subtle highlights

Formula 1
Redken Shades EQ 1/3 7G + 1/3 6WG + 1/3 9AA + Processing Solution

Formula 2
Redken Up to 7 De-Dusted Lightener + 20-volume Pro-oxide Cream Developer

Formula 3
Redken Shades EQ Clear + Processing Solution

Apply Formula 1 to root area and apply Formula 2 to fine weave sections throughout the head. Process and glaze all strands with Formula 3.

87 Chocolate Tone

Naz Kupelian
Rusk Creative Team Member
Naz Kupelian Salon
Boston, MA

Natural Level: 5-7
Target Level: 6 rich, tone-on-tone chocolate shade with dimension and shine.

Formula 1
Rusk Deepshine 5.8 CH + 10-volume developer

Formula 2
Rusk Deepshine 7.8 CH + 8 CH + 10-volume developer

Formula 3
Rusk Deepshine 7.8 + 8 CH + 20-volume developer

Create a zigzag, "beanie" section at the crown of the head. Apply Formula 2 to the beanie parting at the roots. Apply Formula 3 to the ends, and blend colors where they meet in the middle. Apply Formula 1 to all remaining hair. Process 40 minutes.

88

RockMantic Brunette

Robin Sween
Goldwell Educator
Salon Aquivit
Millford, NH

Natural Level: 4-7
Target Level: 6

Formula 1
Goldwell Topchic 15ml 4N + 20ml 4G + 5ml 2A + 40ml 20-volume developer

Formula 2
Goldwell Oxycur Platin Lightening Powder 1 scoop + 35ml 20-volume developer

Formula 3
Goldwell Colorance 3ml 2A + 5ml P Mix + 12ml 10V + 40ml Colorance Intensive Lotion

Formula 4
Goldwell Elumen 10ml PK@all + 3ml RV@all + 1ml BB@all + 30ml AB@9 + 30ml Clear

Formula 5
Goldwell Elumen 20ml BB@all + 20ml NA@2 + 20ml AB@9 + 30ml Clear

Create eight arrows around the head, starting at the arch of each eyebrow, narrowing toward the top of the head. Place a circle at the top of the head. Apply Formula 1 to every other arrow, scalp to ends. Using a compact foiling technique, decolorize alternate arrows with Formula 2. Process to pale yellow, shampoo and condition. Working in alternating slices in the decolorized arrows, apply Formula 1 at the base. Diffuse the first slice with Formula 3. Apply Formula 4 to the second slice, diffuse the third slice with Formula 5, then apply Formula 1 scalp to ends. The last slice is Formula 1 at the base diffused with Formula 5 blended into Formula 4. Apply Formula 1 to the top circle, scalp to ends.

89

Smoky Brunette

Susan Roberts Cooper
TIGI National Creative Technical Director

Natural Level: 5
Existing Level/Shade: 6 with copper tones and one inch of regrowth
Target Result: Dimensional, bitter chocolate brunette flecked with milk chocolate and smoke.

Formula 1
TIGI Colour Radiant Gloss 1 tube 4/0 + 3 inches 0/11 TIGI Colour Mix Master Blue + 3 inches 0/77 Mix Master Dark Ash + 8.5-volume TIGI Colour Activator

Formula 2
TIGI Colour Creative 6/1 + 20-volume TIGI Colour Activator

Formula 3
TIGI Colour Creative 1 tube 8/1 + 1 inch 0/11 TIGI Colour Mix Master Blue + 2 inches 0/77 TIGI Colour Mix Master Dark Ash + 20-volume TIGI Colour Activator

Create a halo shape on top of the head incorporating the crown and clip away the section. Create a crescent shape at the front of the head underneath the halo from one side of the head shape to the other, including the fringe and high recession, with the point of the crescent above the ear. Clip securely. The remaining hair forms the final section.

Apply Formula 1 to the unsecured back and perimeter sections, root area first, then extending the color to midlengths and ends. Isolate with TIGI Colour Meche Strips. Apply Formula 1 to the halo section, roots first and then extend to midlengths and ends. Apply Formula 1 to the root area of the crescent shape. Starting on one side of the shape, create a fine diagonal forward slice and apply Formula 2 to midlengths and ends. Isolate with a strip. Create a second fine diagonal forward slice and apply Formula 3 to midlengths and ends. Isolate with a strip. Create a third diagonal section and apply Formula 1. Repeat, alternating the three formulas until the crescent shape is complete. Process 35 minutes.

90 Dark Chocolate

Maria Guasta
Rusk Creative Team

Natural Level: 6
Target Level: 6 dark chocolate with caramel lights

Formula 1
Rusk DeepShine 20g 5.8ch + 20g 6.3g + 60 grams 10-volume developer

Formula 2
Rusk DeepShine 30g 7.8ch + 10 g 7.03nl + 60g 30-volume developer

Create two circular, one-inch bands around the head. The first sits under the curve of the crown and extends from back to front; the second begins an inch from the occipital and extends to the front of the head, sitting an inch above the tops of the ears and ending an inch from the front hairline. Apply Formula 1 in back-to-back foils in the first circular section and Formula 2 in the same manner in the second circular section. Process 35 minutes.

91

Cherry Chocolate

Mia Liguori McHugh
Scruples International Haircolor Educator and Vice President of Creative
Lakeville, MN

Natural Level: 3
Target Level: 5 rich, reflective, warm brown

Formula 1
Scruples True Integrity 1-oz. 4MG + 1.5-oz. 20-volume PURE Oxi Crème Developer

Formula 2
Scruples Blazing 2 scoops X-tra Light Booster Concentrate + ¼-oz. 6R + ¼-oz. 6A + ½-oz. Blazing Oil Lightener + 1 ½-oz. 10-volume Pure Oxi 10 Developer

Apply Formula 1 to all strands using a virgin application technique. After the cold shafts have processed for 15 minutes, apply a fresh mixture to the scalp. Apply Formula 2 (highlights) over the wet color to produce a monochromatic, tone-on-tone effect. Process 35 minutes.

92

Copper Treasures

René Antonio
Scruples Artistic Director

Natural Level: 4
Target Level: 4, color treated

Formula 1
Scruples Illusionist Brilliant Creme Highlights 4RV (Crimson) + Scruples Pure Oxi 20-volume Creme Developer

Formula 2
Scruples Illusionist Brilliant Creme Highlights 5CR (Firestorm) + Scruples Pure Oxi 20-volume Creme Developer

Formula 3
Scruples Illusionist Brilliant Creme Highlights 7GN (Gold Coast) + Scruples Illusionist Accelerator Powder + Scruples Pure Oxi 20-volume Creme Developer. Alternate Formulas 1-3 in a star pattern in weave foil sections throughout the top of the head.

Formula 4
Scruples True Integrity Opalescent Color Creme 2N + Scruples Pure Oxi 10-volume Creme Developer.

Apply to all remaining strands. Process 30 minutes.

93

Purple Jewel-Toned Brunette

Maryl Velbeck
National Education Director, Phyto Botanical Hair Care
Subtil Colorante

Natural level: 4-5
Target level: 4-5 with rich royal purple tones

Formula 1
Phyto Subtil Shine Lightening Paste 1:2 + Subtil Shine Oxidante Crème (1:2 ratio)

Formula 2
Phyto Subtil Crème ½-oz. 4-20 Plum Brown + ½-oz. 4 + ¼-oz. Les Basiques Violet + 1 ¾-oz.10-volume Subtil Shine Oxidante Crème

Formula 3
Phyto Subtil Crème ½-oz. 5-20 + ¼-oz. Les Basiques Violet + 1 ½-oz. 10-volume Subtil Shine Oxidante Crème

Create a triangular section at the top of the head, apex to eyebrow. Sub-divide the triangle into 4-6 sections. Backcomb each subsection gently, place in foil and apply Formula 1. Apply Formula 2 to remaining hair. Process 30 minutes, shampoo base color, remove foil and shampoo highlights. Apply Formula 3 to highlighted strands, process 10-20 minutes.

reds

94

Strawberry Blonde

Alexis Unno
Garren Salon
New York, NY

Natural Level: 6-8 with 40-70% grey
Target Level: 7-8

Formula
L'Oreal Majirel 1-oz. 7.3 + 1-oz. 8.3 + 20-volume developer.

Process 35-40 minutes.

95

Sangria Red

Kim Vo
Kim Vo Salons
Las Vegas, NV and Beverly Hills, CA

Natural Level: 5-7
Target Level: 6, cool blue/red

Formula 1
L'Oreal Majirel ½ tube 5N + ½ tube 6.46 + ¼ tube 5.6 + 20-volume developer.

Apply to regrowth.

Formula 2
Redken Shades EQ 6RB + Processing Solution.

Apply to midshafts and ends. Process 30 minutes.

96

Delicious Red

Lucie Doughty
John Paul Mitchell Systems Editorial Director
Los Angeles, CA

Natural Level: 5
Target Level: 4 deep copper with strong red undertones

<u>Formula</u>
Paul Mitchell The Color 1-oz. 6RO + ½-oz. 6RR + 1-oz. 5VR + 2 ½-oz. 30-volume developer.

Apply to all strands; process 35 minutes.

97

Sultry Red

James Edick
Arrojo Studio
New York, NY

Natural/Existing Level: 6
Target Level: 7 rich, sultry, standout color

<u>Formula</u>
Wella Koleston Perfect 7/43 + 7/34 + 20-volume developer.

Process 35 minutes.

Note: Adding Wella Koleston Perfect Super Mix Concentrate 0/43 to the formula will increase the intensity of the color.

98 Beth's' Signature Red

Beth Minardi
BTC Color Education Director
Minardi Salon
New York, NY

Existing level: 4 with less than 50% grey
Target level: 5 warm red

Formula 1
Redken Color Fusion 6BBC.

Apply to regrowth.

Formula 2
Redken Blonde Icing + 40-volume developer for quarterly highlights

Formula 3
Redken Shades EQ 08C + SEQ Processing Solution. Apply to hair shaft.

Note: Wella Color Touch 5/5 + Emulsion 1.9% is used for periodic lowlighting throughout the year.

99

Vintage Red

John Simpson
Goldwell North American Guest Artist
Lewis Salon
McDonald, PA

Natural Level: 6 (or dimensional Level 5)
Target Level: 6 vivid, "vintage" red

Formula
Goldwell Topchic 40ml 20-volume developer + 30ml 6RV + 10m 6SB (silver brown).

Process 35 minutes.

100

Intense Copper

Sue Pemberton
Joico Vero K-PAK International Artistic Director
Las Vegas, NV

Natural Level: 5-7
Target Level: 6 bright, intense copper

Formula
Joico Vero K-PAK ¾ 6RC (Red Copper) + ¼ INC (Copper Intensifier) + 10-to-30-volume developer (depending on the existing level.)

Process 30 minutes.

101

Favorite Red

Kaz Amor
Redken Creative Color Consultant
Warren Tricomi Salon
Los Angeles, CA

Existing Level: 7
Target Level: 7-8 intense, copper red

Formula 1
Redken Color Fusion 9OR + 10-volume developer applied to base.

Formula 2
Redken Shades EQ 9AA + 2 caps Orange Kicker + SEQ Processing Lotion on midlengths and ends.

Process 35 minutes.

102

Magenta

Sue Pemberton
Joico Vero K-PAK International Artistic Director
Las Vegas, NV

Existing Level: 9-10 prelightened blonde
Target Level: 10 strong, modern magenta

Formula
Joico Vero K-PAK Intensifiers Magenta with no developer.

Process 20 minutes or until desired shade is achieved.

103

Vibrant Red

Gina Khan
Logics International Spokesperson
Gina Khan Salon
San Francisco and Walnut Creek, CA.

Existing Level: 4-6
Target Level: 5 deep, vibrant, warm, clear red

<u>Formula 1</u>
Logics Gel Lightener 2-oz. + ½ scoop Light Reactions powder lightener + equal parts 20-volume developer to "clean" hair if necessary.

Start ½ inch away from scalp, allow shaft to process and lighten to an orange 7/8 before applying to scalp area. Process at room temperature and shampoo.

<u>Formula 2</u>
Logics Imprints Demi-Permanent Gelucent Color 2-oz. 4RO FULL (Red Orange) + 1-oz. 6G SHEER (Gold) + 3-oz. 10-volume Color Generator

Apply to scalp area.

<u>Formula 3</u>
Logics Imprints 2-oz. 4RO FULL + 1-oz. 6RO FULL + 3-oz. 10-volume Color Generator

Apply to midlengths and ends.Process 10-15 minutes.

104 Reddish Copper

Marie Robinson
Sally Hershberger Salon
New York, NY

Existing Level: 5-8 (can cover up to 20% grey)
Target Level: 6-7 believable red copper that appears more intense on lighter levels

Formula
Redken Shades EQ 2-oz. 6AA + 1-oz. 8C + ½ oz 6R + 3 ½-oz. Processing Solution.

Process 20 minutes with heat on towel-dried hair. Cool five minutes and remove.

105 Copper Auburn Red

David R. Stanko
Redken Haircolor Consultant
New York, NY

Natural Level: 5 with up to 30% grey
Target Level: 7 rich, vibrant, copper/auburn

Formula
Redken Color Fusion 1 ½-oz. 7Cr + ¼-oz. 8Gr + ¼-oz 6Bc + 2-oz. 20-volume Pro-Oxide developer. Apply to regrowth.

Refresh Glaze
Redken Shades EQ 1-oz. 6AA + 1-oz. 9AA + 2-oz. Processing Solution.

Apply to midlengths and ends. Process the base for 35 minutes and the glaze for 15 minutes, simultaneously.

106

Copper Gold Red

The artists: *Christopher and Sonya Dove*
Wella Creative Directors
The Doves
Santa Monica, CA

Natural Level: 5
Target Level: 7 copper penny red

<u>Formula 1</u>
Wella Koleston Perfect 7/34 (warm copper gold) + 20-volume developer. Apply one inch out from regrowth area.

<u>Formula 2</u>
Wella Koleston Perfect 7/34 (warm copper gold) + 8/34 (copper gold) + 1 inch 0/43 + 20-volume developer.

Apply to all remaining strands. Process 30 minutes.

107

Mahogany Red

Tracey Cunningham
Redken Creative Color Consultant
Byron & Tracey Salon
Beverly Hills, CA

Natural Level: 6-7
Target Level: 6-7

Formula
Redken Shades EQ equal parts 7G + 9AA + 8C + SEQ Processing Lotion.

Process 15 minutes with heat, and an additional five minutes without heat.

108

Intense Red

Sue Pemberton
Joico Vero K-PAK International Artistic Director
Las Vegas, NV

Natural Level: 6-8
Target Level: 6 bright, intense red

Formula
Joico Vero K-PAK ¾ 6RR (Ruby Red) + ¼ INRV (Red Violet Intensifier) + 10-to-30-volume developer (depending on the existing level.)

Process 30 minutes.

109 Copper Red

Patrick McIvor
Matrix Artistic Color Director
Patrick McIvor Color Studios, PA

Natural Level: 5-6/medium-light brown
Target Level: 7-8 rich copper red (dark-medium blonde)

<u>Formula</u>
Matrix SoColor 8CC + 7RR + 1 inch SoRed Red + 20-volume SoLite Cream Developer.

Process 30 minutes.

110 Strawberry Blonde

John Simpson
Goldwell North American Guest Artist
Lewis Salon
McDonald, PA

Natural Level: 6-7
Target Level: 8-9 perfect, vivid, strawberry blonde

<u>Formula</u>
Goldwell Topchic 50ml 30-volume developer + 15ml 11G + 10ml 7RR.

Process 35 minutes.

111

Power Red

Doug MacIntosh
Sahag Workshop
New York, NY

Natural Level: 4-6 with no more than 25% grey
Target Level: 6 rich, believable red

Formula 1
L'Oreal Majirel ½ tube 6.3 + ¼ tube 6.43 + ¼ tube 7.4 + 2.6-oz. Majirel Color Developer. (For increased intensity, add a ribbon of 7.44.) Process 30 minutes, shampoo and dry.

Formula 2
Redken Shades EQ 2-oz. 06C + ½-oz. 08WG + 2 ½-oz. Processing Solution. (For a bolder result, replace the 08WG with Shades EQ Orange Kicker.)

Process with heat for 10 minutes; cool 10 minutes and remove.

112

Red Currant

Christel Lundqvist
British Colour Technician of the Year
hob salons
Great Britain

Natural Level: 5 and higher
Target Level: 6 vibrant, currant red

Formula
Wella Koleston Perfect 55/46 + 0/81 + 6% developer.

Process 30-40 minutes.

113

Coppery Red

Nury Lopez
Rusk Creative Team Member

Natural Level: 7
Existing Level: 6
Target Level: 7 copper/red

Formula
Rusk Deepshine Pure Pigments Conditioning Cream Color 2-oz. 7.44 + 1-oz. 6.66 + 10-volume developer.

Process 35 minutes.

114 *Stunning Red*

Lucus Etcitty
Vidal Sassoon Academy Color Director,
Santa Monica, CA

Natural/Existing Level: 5 virgin color
Target Level: 5 brilliant, multi-tonal, cool red

Formula
Wella Koleston Perfect Intensive Red Series 1-oz. 77/44 + 1-oz. 44/65 + 2-oz. 20-volume developer.

Process 30-40 minutes.

115 *"Debra Messing" Red*

Nancy Braun
Christophe Salon, Beverly Hills, CA and
Roy Teeluck Salon, New York, NY

Natural Level: 5-6
Target Level: 7 vibrant yet believable red

Formula 1
L'Oreal Luocolor ¾ tube 7.46 + ¼ tube 7.40 + 20-volume developer. Apply roots to ends, process 30 minutes.

Formula 2 (optional)
L'Oreal Majimeche + 20-volume developer.

Apply balayage highlights around the face; process to soft, golden copper (approximately 10 minutes.)

116

Vibrant Red

David Adams
RedCHOCOLATE
Minneapolis, MN

Natural Level: 5 light brown
Target Level: 5 vibrant red

Formula 1
Aveda Full Spectrum 20g Dark Pure Base + 20g 5N + 6g Red/Orange Pure Tone + 4g Dark Yellow/Orange Pure tone + 40g 20-volume Color Catalyst. Apply to new growth.

Formula 2
Aveda Full Spectrum 40g Dark Pure Base + 8g Red/Orange Pure Tone + 2g Yellow Orange Pure Tone + 40g 30-volume Color Catalyst.

Apply to midlengths and ends.

117

Redwood

Teri Dougherty
Wella Guest Artist
San Francisco, CA

Natural Level: 4-8
Target Level: 6 rich, vibrant, natural redwood

Formula
Wella Koleston Perfect 6/74 + 6/75 + 20-volume developer.
(For lighter results: Wella Koleston Perfect 8/74 + 6/75 + 20-volume developer.)

Process 30-40 minutes.

118

Fiery Sunset

Mia Liguori McHugh
Scruples International Haircolor Educator and Vice President of Creative
Lakeville, MN

Natural Level: 6
Existing Level: 6 with highlighted ends
Target Level: 7

<u>Formula</u>
Scruples High Definition Color Gel 1-oz. 6RR + 1-oz. 8G + 2-oz. 10-volume Pure Oxi Clear Developer.

Process 30 minutes.

119

No Apologies Red

René Antonio
Scruples Artistic Director

Natural Level: 6
Existing Level: 6 with 20% existing highlights
Target Result: Brilliant, full-bodied red with a combination of warm and cool tones

Formula 1
Scruples Illusionist Brilliant Creme Highlights 4R (Scarlet) + Scruples Pure Oxi 20-volume Creme Developer

Formula 2
Scruples Illusionist Brilliant Creme Highlights 5CO (Burning Ambition) + Scruples Pure Oxi 20- volume Creme Developer

Formula 3
Scruples Illusionist Brilliant Creme Highlights 7GN (Gold Coast) + Scruples Illusionist Accelerator Powder + Scruples Pure Oxi 20-volume Creme Developer. Alternate Formulas 1-3 using a "veiled" highlighting technique throughout crown area.

Formula 4
Scruples True Integrity Opalescent Colour Crème 6RR (Radiant Red) + Scruples Pure Oxi 10-volume Creme Developer. Apply to new growth.

Formula 5
Scruples True Integrity Opalescent Colour Crème 6RR (Radiant Red) + Scruples Pure Oxi 20-volume Creme Developer.

Apply to lengths. Process 30 minutes.

120

Favorite Red

Anita Gutierrez
Clairol Professional Color Master and Educator
Backyard Day Spa
Long Beach, CA

Existing Level: 3-4
Target Level: 3-6

Formula 1
Clairol Professional Premium Crème 1 ½-oz. 3RR + ¾-oz. 1N + 20-volume developer. Place within a diamond-shaped section at the top of the head.

Formula 2
Clairol Professional 1 ½-oz. 6RR + ½-oz. 8G + 20-volume developer.

Apply to remaining strands. Process 35 minutes.

121 Copper Zap

Brian & Sandra Smith
Matrix Artistic Designers
Dalton, GA

Natural/ Existing Level: 5 (base) and 8-9 (midlengths and ends)
Target Level: 4, deep, red/brown with an orange/copper accent

Formula 1
Matrix Color Sync Seamless Crème Demi-Color 2-oz. 6RC + 2-oz. Activator. Working back 1 ½-inch from the hairline, create a triangle and clip. Section the rest of the head into quadrants and apply to midlengths and ends. Process 10 minutes. Remove and dry hair 80%.

Formula 2
Matrix Prizms.Plus Semi-Permanent Hyper Shine Color Gloss 1-oz. Intense Orange + 1/8-oz. Zappy Red

Formula 3
Matrix Color Sync Seamless Crème Demi-Color 2-oz. 4RB + 2-oz. Activator.

Re-section triangle and apply Formula 3 ½-inch to ¾-inch from the scalp within the triangle section.

Apply Formula 2 to midlengths and ends. Section remaining hair into quadrants and apply Formula 3 from scalp to ends. Process 10-20 minutes.

122

Show-Stopping Copper

Michael Elving
Affinage National Artistic Educational Director
Las Vegas, NV

Natural Level: 5
Target Level: 5-6 fashion-forward copper

Formula 1
Affinage Infiniti 2.2 + 10-volume developer

Formula 2
Affinage Infiniti 4.2 + 10-volume developer

Formula 3
Affinage Infiniti 6.66 + 10-volume developer

Formula 4
Affinage Infiniti ¾ 7.43 + ¼ Copper B-Red + 10 volume developer

Apply Formula 1 to all strands below the occipital. On top sections, alternate Formula 2 and 3 in weave foil sections. Apply Formula 4 between the weaves. Process 45 minutes.

123

Crown Jewel

Lucie Doughty
John Paul Mitchell Systems Editorial Director,
Los Angeles, CA

Natural Level: 4-6
Target Level: 6 rich, overlaying hues of cool and warm red

Formula 1
Paul Mitchell The Color PM Shines 1-oz. 6RO + 3 shots Color Shots Red + 1-oz. Processing Liquid

Formula 2
Paul Mitchell The Color PM Shines 1-oz. 6R + 3 shots Color Shots Red + 1-oz. Processing Liquid

Divide the head into three horizontal sections. The first section is a ½-inch section around the hairline. The second/middle section is horseshoe-shaped and drapes over the middle. It must be large enough to accommodate two diamonds and four triangles. Apply Formula 2 to the first section and overlay with foil. Apply Formula 1 to the middle section. Alternate Formulas 1 and 2 within diamond and triangles shapes in the top section. Process 20 minutes.

124

Rich Garnet Red

Dhaniel Doud
Redken Haircolor Consultant

Natural Level: 3-5
Target Level: 5 rich blend of cool and warm red/browns

Formula 1
Redken Shades EQ 5Mv Teak + Processing Solution

Formula 2
Redken Color Fusion 1-oz. 5Rc + 1-oz. 20-volume Pro-Oxide

Formula 3
Redken Color Fusion ½-oz. 6Mv + ½-oz. 6Rv + 1-oz. 20-volume Pro-Oxide

Create a medium-sized diamond at the top of the head and secure. All sides should be equal. Using each corner as a reference point, create a square and secure for a total of four squares. Beginning in the back square, create a fine slice, apply Formula 1 from scalp down one inch and apply Formula 2 to remaining hair. Continue working in this manner on fine slices. As work progresses, extend the application of Formula 1 slightly. Repeat on all square sections. Create a fine slice on the diamond section and apply Formula 1 from scalp down one inch and Formula 3 to remaining hair. Continue throughout the entire section. Process 30-35 minutes.

125

Red Diffusion

Deborah Gavin
Goldwell North American Guest Artist
Southampton, PA

Existing Level: 7
Target Result: A versatile red that can be subtle or bright

<u>Formula 1</u>
Goldwell Pre Pigmentation System 60 mls water + 20mls Red + 10 mls Copper.

<u>Formula 2</u>
Goldwell Topchic 20mls 7KR + 10mls 9KG + 5mls 6RO + 5mls 8RO + 40mls 20-volume developer.

Working through the flats and rounds of the head, create 2 x 2-inch subsections and clip. Create and isolate five subsections throughout the head shape and apply Formula 1 to all remaining hair. Apply Formula 2 over the Formula 1 pre-pigmenter.

<u>Formula 3</u>
Goldwell Topchic 30mls 3VR + 30mls 10-volume developer.

<u>Formula 4</u>
Goldwell Elumen 20mls GK@All + 5mls PK@All + 5mls YY@All. Create ¼-inch, back-to-back slices within the original subsections.

Apply Formula 3 at the base of each slice, and softly blend the color outward with the side of the brush. Apply Formula 4 to the ends of the same slices. Process 30 minutes.

126

Antique Strawberry

Berry Bachen
TIGI Academy
New York, NY

Natural Level: 6 or higher
Target Level: 7-8

<u>Formula 1</u>
Equal parts TIGI Colour Creative 7/4 + TIGI Colour Creative 10/0 + 1-in. TIGI Colour MixMaster 0/22 + 2-in.TIGI Colour MixMaster + 20-volume Activator (base color).

<u>Formula 2</u>
TIGI Colour UltraLift 100+/0 + 4-in. TIGI Colour MixMaster 0/33 + 1-in. TIGI Colour MixMaster 0/66 + 30-volume Activator

<u>Formula 3</u>
TIGI Colour Modern Lightener + 4-in. TIGI Colour Lights Saffron + 1-in. TIGI Colour Lights Iris + 20-volume Activator (alternate formulas 2 and 3 as foil highlights.)

127

Dark, Vibrant Red

Maria Guasta
Rusk Creative Team Member

Natural Level: 6
Existing Level: 8 with a pink cast
Target Level: 7 rich, saffron red

Formula 1
Rusk Deepshine Pure Pigments Conditioning Cream Color 40g 7.43cg + 40g Balanced Lotion. Fill all strands with this formula, process 20 minutes and remove pigment with a towel.

Formula 2
Rusk Deepshine Pure Pigments Conditioning Cream Color 40g 7.44 + 60g 10-volume developer.

Process 40 minutes.

128

Copper Pennies

Linda Yodice and Scott Cole
Paul Mitchell Hair Color Artistic Directors
Scottsdale, AZ and Atlanta, GA, Scottsdale, AZ

Natural Level: 5
Target Level: 6

Formula 1
Paul Mitchell The Color 1-oz 5CC + 1-oz. 20-volume Clear Developer

Formula 2
Paul Mitchell The Color 1-oz. 6CC + 1-oz. 30-volume Clear Developer

Formula 3
Paul Mitchell The Color 1-oz. 7CC + 1-oz. 30-volume Clear Developer

Create a horseshoe-shaped section from recession to recession, on the round of the head. Secure with a clip. Apply Formula 2 to the hair below the round. Move to the top section and create a circular section, beginning at the center/back. Using a beveled sponge, apply Formula 1. Subsection as necessary. Create another circular section to the left side of the previous section and apply Formula 2. Continue working on the left side of the head, create the next circular section and apply Formula 2. Continue creating circular sections on the left side, working towards the face and alternate formulas 1, 3 and 2 in this order, finishing with Formula 2 in the center front. Work the right side in the same manner and alternate formulas 3, 2 and 1 in this order meeting at the previously-colored center front section. Return to the starting point. Create another circular section inside the already colored perimeter and just left of the center back. Apply Formula 2. Continue creating circular shaped sections and alternate formulas 1, 2 and 3 inside the perimeter. Once you have finished creating all the circular sections, apply Formula 2 to the scalp area in between the "copper pennies." Process 35 minutes.

129

Fiery Red

Silas Tsang
Blushes Hair & Day Spa
NAHA Color Finalist
Ottawa, ON

Existing Level: 7
Target Level: 6 vivid red

Formula
L'Oreal Majirouge ¾ tube 6.6 + ¼ tube Majirouge Mix Red 0.600 + 20-volume developer.

Process 30 minutes.

formulas that “saved your life”

130

Kristin Stewart's Reverse Burgundy

Stuart Gavert
Gavert Atelier
Beverly Hills, CA

Natural Level: 6
Existing Level: 4 burgundy
Target Level: 6 warm brown

Formula 1
Redken Blonde Icing + 20-volume developer. Apply to entire head in 1/8-inch, back-to-back foiled sections. Process until hair lightens to Level 7.

Formula 2
Redken Shades EQ 1-oz. 9AA + 1-oz. 8WG with no Processing Solution. Apply to ends.

Formula 3
Redken Shades EQ 3-oz. 6NB + 3-oz. Processing Solution.

Apply to remaining strands. Process 10 minutes.

131 Gray Standard

Davin Dawson
Tom Brophy Salon
Beverly Hills, CA

Natural Level: 6 with 60% grey
Existing Level: 9/10 on ends
Target Level: 9.5 natural gold
Correction goal: To produce even coverage after the client received Japanese thermal straightening treatment which prevented grey hair from absorbing color because cuticles were too wide open.

Formula 1
Goldwell Topchic 15mls 11A + 15ml 9N + 10mls 8N plus 40mls 30-volume developer

Process 45 minutes.

Formula 2
Goldwell Colorance 15mls 9GB + 15mls 8GB + 60mls Processing Lotion.

Process 20 minutes.

132 Remove Unwanted Tone

Nelson Chan
Nelson J. Salon
Beverly Hills, CA

Correction goal: Reverse a color that appears too dark or exhibits unwanted tone.

<u>Formula</u>
Perform clarifying shampoo, followed by Malibu 2000 Crystal Gel Normalizer or Nelson J. Detox Crystal.

Apply heat for 5-10 minutes, re-shampoo with deep cleansing formula.

133 Lighten up the Black

Christel Lundqvist
British Colour Technician of the Year
hob Salons
Great Britain

Existing Level: 3 or darker
Correction Goal: Produce lighter color on black hair with heavy build-up.

<u>Formula</u>
Wella Magma 89+ with 9% or 12% developer.

Process until desired level is attained. Tone with desired formula.

134

Get Rid of Unwanted Tones

Lisa Marie Garcia
Farouk Systems Show Department Director
Houston, TX

Correction goal: Correct unwanted tones or refresh drab color.

<u>Formula</u>
Choose from 10 shades of CHI Organics Tone & Shine Enhancing Conditioners.

Apply to all strands. Process 5-15 minutes.

135

Bright Orange Fix

Gina Khan
Logics International Spokesperson
Gina Khan Salon
San Francisco and Walnut Creek, CA

Natural/Existing Level: 7 medium blonde
Correction goal: Light, cool results with no trace of orange undertones.

<u>Formula 1</u>
Logics Light Reactions 1 ½ scoops + 1-oz. Gel Lightener + 20-volume Color Generator.

<u>Formula 2</u>
Logics Imprints Demi-Permanent 1-oz. 6RB SHEER (blue) + 2-oz. 8B SHEER (Blue) + 5-volume Color Generator.

Highlight approximately 30 percent of hair, concentrating on areas around the face, on the surface and behind the ear, with Formula 1. Process at room temperature. When hair in the foil reaches the yellow stage, apply Formula 2 between foils. Process an additional 15 minutes.

136

Remove Unwanted Tones

Marie Robinson
Sally Hershberger Salon
New York, NY

Correction goal: Remove color that is too dark, too red or too ashy and prepare hair for subsequent color application.

Formula
L'Oreal Diacolor 1 part Clear + 2 parts 15-volume developer.

Process 5-15 minutes depending on amount of color to be removed.

137

Bring Back the Light

David R. Stanko
Redken Haircolor Consultant
New York, NY

Natural Level: 4
Existing Color Situation: Hair was highlighted, then over-glazed, causing highlights to disappear.
Correction Goal: Restore hair to a soft, lightest brown with dark blonde highlights.

Formula
Redken Shimmer One equal parts Clear + 30-volume Pro-Oxide Developer.

Apply off-scalp to all hair using a four-section blocking and fine partings. Fully saturate each strand. Process 7-10 minutes.

138

Knock Down the Blonde

Christopher and Sonya Dove
Wella Creative Directors
The Doves Salon
Santa Monica, CA

Correction Goal: Darken over-lightened blonde to a soft caramel shade.

Formula
Wella Color Touch Demi Permanent 1-oz. 6/77 (Milk Chocolate) + 1-oz. 9/3 (Very Light Golden Blonde) + 1-oz. 7/73 (Warm Caramel) + double Color Touch Emulsion 1.9%.

Can apply as lowlights or full-head application on damp, clean hair. Process up to 30 minutes.

139

Amber Blonde

Jonathan Gale
SoloArtists.com
Chris McMillan Salon
Beverly Hills, CA

Existing Level: 7 with a "tobacco" cast
Target Result: Warm amber brown without a trace of green

Formula
Paul Mitchell PM Shines 9RO + Processing Liquid

Apply to all strands, process five minutes.

140

Gold Filler

Alexis Unno
Garren Salon
New York, NY

Correction Goal: Gold filler for blonde hair.

<u>Formula</u>
10 drops of Ardell Lock-In Blonde per 1-oz. of warm water.

Apply to hair and then apply color directly over filler. Process per manufacturer's instructions.

141

Golden Tones

Clark Wood
Garren Salon
New York, NY

Target Level/Goal: Level 5 or lighter golden tones without brassiness.

<u>Formula</u>
L'Oreal Diacolor Gelee 1 part Gold + 1 part Clear + 2 parts developer.

Process 5-15 minutes.

142

Warm Brown Recovery

Kazumi Morton
Eiji Salon
New York, NY

Natural Level: 7
Target Level: 6
Correction Goal: Enhance faded tones and restore a rich, warm hue.

Formula 1
Redken Color Fusion 1-oz. BBr + 1-oz. 6MV + 2-oz. 20-volume developer. Apply to regrowth. Process 35 minutes.

Formula 2
Redken Shades EQ 1-oz. 6WG + 1-oz. 6MV + 2-oz. Processing Solution.

Apply to midlengths and ends for final 15 minutes of total processing time.

143

Second Nature

Anita Gutierrez
Clairol Professional Color Master and Educator
Backyard Day Spa
Long Beach, CA

Natural Level: 5 or 6
Existing Color Situation: Very white color that will not hold pigment.

Formula
Clairol Professional Premium Crème 1 ½-oz. 6N + ½-oz. 5R + 2-oz. 10 volume developer.

Process 35-40 minutes.

144

Red Copper

Brian & Sandra Smith
Matrix Artistic Designers
Dalton, GA

Natural Level: 5
Midlengths and Ends: 9-10 overly blonde with spots
Target Result: Transform over-lightened hair to a rich, red copper

Formula 1
Matrix Color Sync 2-oz. 6RC + 2-oz. Activator

Formula 2
Matrix Color Sync 1 ½-oz. 4RB + ½-oz. 6RC + 2-oz. Activator

Section hair into quadrants and apply Formula 1 to midlengths and ends. Process 10 minutes, rinse thoroughly and dry hair 80%. Re-section into quadrants and apply Formula 2 scalp to ends. Process 10-20 minutes depending on hair porosity.

145

Fashion Forward Blonde

Deborah Gavin
Goldwell North American Guest Artist
Fresh Hair Studio
Southampton, PA

Existing Level: 8G
Target Result: A cool, "fashion-forward" blonde

<u>Formula 1</u>
Goldwell Oxy Ultra + 10-volume developer. Apply to all strands to "clean the canvas." Process 15 minutes.

<u>Formula 2</u>
Goldwell Topchic 40mls 10-volume developer + 25mls 6A + 2mls 2A + 13mls 10A

<u>Formula 3</u>
Goldwell Topchic 20mls 10-volume developer + 10mls 9RV + 25mls 10A + 5mls 6A + 20mls water.

Create a star-shaped section on the top of the head and alternate slices of Formulas 2 and 3 within the section. Process and remove.

146

Orange Fix

Doug MacIntosh
Sahag Workshop
New York, NY

Natural/Existing Level: 7 with intense orange bleeding
Target Result/Correction Goal: Remove hot "bleed" marks and produce a more natural-looking blonde.

<u>Formula 1</u>
L'Oreal Richesse 1 tube 6 + Richesse 9-volume developer.
Apply to regrowth, process 30 minutes, shampoo, condition and dry hair thoroughly.

<u>Formula 2</u>
Clairol BW2 Powder Lightener + 10-volume developer. Place high at the roots using a horizontal foil pattern. Process until roots match the ends.

<u>Formula 3</u>
L'Oreal Diacolor Gelee 1-oz. Light Golden Blonde + 2-oz. Diacolor developer.

Apply at the sink; process five minutes.

147

Brassy Recovery

Kazumi Morton
Eiji Salon
New York, NY

Natural Level: 3
Target Level: 6
Correction goal: Subdue brassy midshaft and end undertones common in Asian and Hispanic hair types.

<u>Formula 1</u>
Redken Color Fusion 1-oz. 7T + 1-oz. 6Ag + 2-oz. 20-volume developer. Apply to regrowth for 40 minutes.

<u>Formula 2</u>
Redken Shades EQ 1-oz. 6GN + 1-oz. 7T + 2-oz. Processing Solution.

Apply to midlengths and ends for final five minutes of total processing time.

148 From Blonde to Dark Brown

Ellie Coates
Arrojo Studio
New York, NY

Existing Level: 5-6 with 8-9 highlights
Target Level/Result: 6 rich brunette without "muddiness"

Formula 1
Wella Color Touch 6/1 + 1.9% Emulsion

Formula 2
Wella Color Touch 4/77 and 6/77 with 4% Emulsion

Apply Formula 1 to new growth, apply Formula 2 to all remaining hair, including roots. Process up to 30 minutes.

149 Bringing Down the Blonde

Patrick McIvor
Matrix Artistic Color Director
Patrick McIvor Color Studios
PA

Natural Level/Starting Level: 8-9 medium/light blonde
Target Level: 7 dark blonde
Correction goal: Bring an overprocessed tone to Level 7 without a muddy appearance.

<u>Formula</u>
Matrix Color Sync 3 parts 7WN + 1 part 7MM + equal parts Color Sync Activator.

(Can be used as a lowlight or as all-over color.) Process up to 20 minutes.

150 Brighten up your Brown

Tracey Cunningham
Byron and Tracey Salon
Redken Creative Color Consultant
Beverly Hills, CA

Existing Level: 6, dull brown
Target Level: 7
Correction Goal: Brighten, add shine, even out the tone

<u>Formula 1</u>
Redken Up to 7. Apply this “bleach wash” to all strands and process.

<u>Formula 2</u>
Redken Shades EQ 20cc 9NB + 30cc Clear + 20cc 9B + Processing Solution.

Glaze all strands.

151

Removing Excess Tint

John Simpson
Goldwell North American Guest Artist
Lewis Salon
McDonald, PA

Existing Level: 5 red
Correction Goal: Clean the "canvas" of excess tint and introduce a new tonal shade without performing a bleach and tone.

Formula 1
50ml 40-volume developer + 20 ml Goldwell Blonding Cream + 5mls KK Goldwell Mix Shade

Formula 2
50ml 40 volume developer + 23 ml Goldwell Blonding Cream Ash + 2 ml RR Goldwell Mix Shade. Alternate Formulas 1 and 2 throughout to produce highlights.

Formula 3
Goldwell Colorance 9KG.

Overlay all strands. Process up to 50 minutes to highlight and tone in a single step.

152

Getting Even

René Antonio
Scruples Artistic Director

Existing Shade: Level 4 regrowth; golden midshaft; blonde ends
Target Result: Level 4 cherry chocolate

Formula 1
Scruples Blazing Lowlights 4GN + 7GR + Scruples Pure Oxi 10-volume Clear Developer. Apply to midshafts and ends to fill hair.

Formula 2
Scruples True Integrity Opalescent Color Creme 4MG (Cherry Chocolate) + Scruples Pure Oxi 10-volume Creme Developer. Apply to new growth.

Formula 3
Scruples True Integrity Opalescent Color Creme 4MG (Cherry Chocolate) + Scruples Pure Oxi Demi-Permanent Creme Developer.

Apply to midshafts and ends.

153

Outdated to Outstanding

Mia Liguori McHugh
Scruples International Haircolor Educator and Vice President of Creative
Lakeville, MN

Natural Level: 7
Existing Level: 10 midshafts and ends
Target Level: 8

Formula 1
Scruples Blazing 1-oz. 7GR + 10-volume Pure Oxi Developer

Formula 2
Scruples Blazing 1-oz. 6GN + 10-volume Pure Oxi Developer

Formula 3
Scruples Blazing 4GN + 10-volume Pure Oxi Developer

Formula 4 (Highlights)
Scruples 2 scoops Blazing X-tra Light Booster Concentrate + ¼-oz. 8G + ¼-oz. 10A + ½-oz. Blazing Oil Lightener + 1 ½-oz. 20-volume Pure Oxi Clear Developer

Alternate all formulas in back-to-back foil slices, beginning at the side of the head. Work in diagonal slices across the top of the head and down to the other side to the nape. Apply slices on the other side to the occipital. Add four alternating slices to the fringe. Apply Formula 3 to all hair left out of foils. Process 30 minutes. When rinsing highlights, use cool water and rinse each foil individually to avoid bleeding.

154

Gorgeous Coppery Red

Nury Lopez
Rusk Creative Team Member

Natural Level: 3
Existing Level: 9
Target Level: 7

Formula 1
Rusk Deepshine Pure Pigments Conditioning Cream Color 7.64 + 10-volume developer. Apply as a filler to all strands.

Formula 2
Rusk Deepshine Pure Pigments Conditioning Cream Color 7.44 + 10-volume developer.

Apply directly over Formula 1. Process 35 minutes.

155

Bringing It Down to Brown

Nancy Braun
Christophe Salon, Beverly Hills, CA and
Roy Teeluck Salon, New York, NY

Natural Level: 9-10 (minimal damage)
Target Level: 6 beautiful warm light brown

Formula 1
L'Oreal Majirel ¾ tube 6.3 + ¼ tube 7.4 + 9-volume developer

Formula 2
L'Oreal Diacolor ¾ medium brown + ¼ light ash brown + 9-volume developer

Apply Formula 1 to all areas that are Level 9-10, saturating evenly. Process 25-35 minutes. Apply Formula 2 scalp to ends. Process 20-30 minutes.

avant garde

156

Full Spectrum (COVER FORMULA)

René Antonio
Scruples Artistic Director

Existing Level: 6 at new growth with 30% pre-existing golden highlights
Target Result: A rainbow of fantasy color!

Formula 1
Scruples Power Blonde Hair Lightener + Scruples Pure Oxi 20-volume Creme Developer. Prelighten desired strands. Process 30 minutes.

Formula 2
Scruples Urban Shock Color Craze Purple (no developer required)

Formula 3
Scruples Urban Shock Color Craze Yellow (no developer required)

Formula 4
Scruples Urban Shock Color Craze Orange (no developer required)

Formula 5
Scruples Urban Shock Color Craze Hot Pink (no developer required)

Apply Formulas 2-5 on select strands, using a “blurring” technique. Process 15 minutes at room temperature.

Blue/Black

Gina Khan
Logics International Spokesperson
Gina Khan Salon
San Francisco and Walnut Creek, CA

Existing Level: 3-5
Target Result: inky black

Formula 1
Logics Light Reactions Powder Lightener 2 scoops + 20-volume Color Generator

Formula 2
Logics Color Cremes Permanent Color 3-oz. 1B + 1-oz. Primary Blue Concentrate + 10-volume Color Generator

Formula 3
1-oz. Logics Primary Blue Concentrate + ½-oz. Logics Imprints Clear + 10-volume Color Generator

Weave fine and bold pieces beneath the part line and behind the hairline, (approximately 25-30 foils, some back-to-back) and apply Formula 1 to foil weaves. Apply Formula 2 between foils. Process foils to pale yellow, 20 minutes. Rinse Formula 2 until water runs clear then remove foils and continue rinsing. Shampoo. Apply Formula 3 to prelightened sections. Process 10-15 minutes.

158

Deep Violet Fringe

Alexis Unno
Garren Salon
New York, NY

Existing Level: Can be used on any level; must pre-lighten hair if it is colored.
Target Result: A pop of color for fringes that doesn't go over the top!

Formula
L'Oreal Hi-Richesse 4.26 + 30-volume developer.

Apply to a ¼-inch section along the face frame and process according to manufacturer's instructions.

159

Backcomb Blonde

Christopher John
Garren Salon
New York, NY

Existing Level: Can be used on any base
Target Result: Beautiful blonde on short, layered cuts—best on hair no longer than four inches

Formula
Clairol Basic White + 30-volume developer.

Backcomb random sections and apply lightener. Process 20 minutes.

160

Extreme Contrast

Clark Wood
Garren Salon
New York, NY

Existing Level: 50% grey or more
Target result: High contrast brown/blonde

Formula 1
L'Oreal Majirel 9N + 20-volume developer

Formula 2
L'Oreal Majirel 5N + 20-volume developer

Create block-pattern foils throughout crown area and apply Formula 1. Apply Formula 2 to all remaining hair.

161

Tangerine Tantrums

Kim Vo
Kim Vo Salons
Las Vegas, NV and Beverly Hills, CA

Existing Level: 6-8
Target result: A funky orange hue

Formula 1
L'Oreal Majirel 1 tube 8/43 + ½ 8N + 20-volume developer.

Formula 2
Redken Shades EQ ½ 9AA + ½ 8C + Processing Solution

Apply Formula 1, process and remove and glaze with Formula 2.

162

Uncomplicated Streaks

David R. Stanko
Redken Haircolor Consultant
New York, NY

Target result: Random lightened pieces

<u>Formula 1</u>
2 scoops Redken Up to 7 Powder Lightener + 10-volume Pro-Oxide

<u>Formula 2</u>
2 scoops Redken Up to 7 Powder Lightener + 20-volume Pro-Oxide

<u>Formula 3</u>
Redken Shades EQ equal parts 9GB + 9V + Clear + Processing Solution

Using 12 x 12 plastic sheets, alternate Formulas 1 and 2 in random sections throughout the head. Process to desired level. Glaze with Formula 3.

163

Kaleidoscope of Color

Christopher and Sonya Dove
Wella Creative Directors
The Doves Salon
Santa Monica, CA

Natural Level: 6

Target Level/Effect: 6 with a kaleidoscope of highlights in a heavy weave formation. The lighter areas will be vibrant; the natural hair between the highlights will accept a minimal tone for a deeper kaleidoscope effect.

<u>Formula 1</u>

Wella Koleston Perfect 3 parts Supermix 0/43 (red orange) + 1 part 10/0 Lightest Blonde + Pastel Developer mixed in a 1:2 ratio.

<u>Formula 2</u>

Wella Koleston Perfect 3 parts Supermix 0/65 (violet pink) + 1 part 10/0 Lightest Blonde + Pastel Developer mixed in a 1:2 ratio.

<u>Formula 3:</u>

Wella Koleston Perfect 3 parts Supermix 0/45 (red violet) + 1 part 10/0 Lightest Blonde + Pastel Developer mixed in a 1:2 ratio.

On the lower half of the head, create heavy, vertical, back-to-back slices and alternate each formula, creating a fan effect with the foil. Continue working throughout the head in this manner. Process and remove.

164

Pink Goes Pop

Ellie Coates
Arrojo Studio
New York, NY

Existing Level: Any

Formula
Wella Magma Ultra Lifting Powder Formula 8 parts /89 + 2 parts /56 + developer of choice

Apply directly to strands or in foiled section. Process to desired shade.

165

Pale Pink

Lucie Doughty
John Paul Mitchell Systems Editorial Director
Los Angeles, CA

Existing Level: Pre-lightened
Target result: Pale pink tones

Formula
Paul Mitchell The Color 2-oz. 10N + 1/8-oz. 3VR + 2-oz. 10-volume developer.

Process 10 minutes.

166

Pixilated Red

Kris Sorbie
Redken Education Artistic Director
New York, NY

Natural Level: 4
Target Level: 6 multi-dimensional red tones offset by disconnected design elements

Formula 1 (Dark)
Redken Hi-Fusion 1-oz. Vr + 1-oz. 30-volume Pro-Oxide Developer

Formula 2 (Medium)
Redken Hi-Fusion 1-oz. Rc + 1-oz. 30-volume Pro-Oxide Developer

Formula 3 (Light)
Redken Double Fusion Reds 1-oz. Cr + 2-oz. 30-volume Pro-Oxide Developer

Create varied rectangular sections throughout the head. Alternate each formula within the rectangles. Select one of the three formulas (dark, medium or light) to serve as the base color. Process 35 minutes.

167

Red Pearl

John Simpson
Goldwell North American Guest Artist
Lewis Salon
McDonald, PA

Existing Level: 8-9 prelightened
Target Result: Beautiful, cool red great for enhancing a copper shade or for cooling off Level 7 brunette or making reds and browns pop!

Formula
Goldwell Elumen 60ml AB @ 9 + 3ml Pk @ ALL + 2 ml YY @ ALL.

Process until desired tone is achieved.

168

Backcomb Blonde

Christopher John
Garren Salon
New York, NY

Existing Level: Can be used on any base
Target Result: Beautiful blonde on short, layered cuts—best on hair no longer than four inches

Formula
Clairol Basic White + 30-volume developer.

Backcomb random sections and apply lightener. Process 20 minutes.

169

Softly Bold Color

Deborah Gavin
Goldwell North American Guest Artist
Fresh Hair Studio
Southampton, PA

Natural Level: 5
Target Result: Diffused design via diagonal placement

Formula 1
Goldwell Oxy Ultra + 10 volume developer

Formula 2
Goldwell Elumen YY@ALL

Formula 3
Goldwell Elumen NB@5 + BB@ALL

Create a one-inch zig-zag shape between the flat and round of the head shape. Decolorize this section with Formula 1. Re-isolate the section and apply Formula 2. Apply Formula 3 all around the panel. Process 20 minutes.

170

Manic Panic Loyalist

Doug MacIntosh
Sahag Workshop
New York, NY

Existing Level: Pre-lightened
Target Result: Bold, intense slashes of color

Formula 1
Clairol BW2 Powder Lightener + 40-volume developer

Formula 2
Manic Panic Rock-N-Roll Red or Vampire Red or Hot, Hot Pink or Pillarbox Red or color of your choice.

Apply Formula 1 balayage style to select strands. Process, shampoo and dry completely. Apply Formula 2 to decolorized strands, applying color thickly for maximum vibrancy. Process under heat with no cap until product dries and hardens. Rinse and condition with oil-free moisturizer (oil will remove the direct dyes.)

171

Deep Violet Red

Nelson Chan
Nelson J. Salon
Beverly Hills, CA

Natural Level: 4-6
Target Level/Result: 5-6 ash brown base with accents of deep violet red

Formula 1
Aveda Full Spectrum Deposit Only Color Treatment 40g #5 + 2g BG

Formula 2
Aveda Full Spectrum Dark Pure Base + 2g RV Pure Tone + 20-volume developer

Isolate a section around the parting. Create foil sections beneath the section and apply Formula 2. Apply Formula 1 to all remaining strands. Process 30 minutes.

172

Copper Red Violet

Lucus Etcitty
Vidal Sassoon Academy Color Director
Santa Monica, CA

Natural Level: 5
Existing Level: 5
Target Level: 6-7 violet brown with a copper red panel

<u>Formula 1</u>
Wella Koleston Perfect 7/4 + 20-volume developer

<u>Formula 2</u>
Wella Koleston Perfect 1-oz. 6/77 + 1-oz. 4/6 + 4-oz. 1.9% developer

Create an oblong panel from the middle of the right eye to the left ear. Apply Formula 1 in back-to-back slices within the panel. Apply Formula 2 to all remaining strands. Process 30 minutes.

173

Blonde + Copper

Nury Lopez
Rusk Creative Team Member

Natural Level: 8
Existing Level: 9
Target Level: 8 pale blonde with copper/brown lowlights

<u>Formula 1</u>
Rusk Deepshine Pure Pigments Conditioning Cream Color 6.4 + 10-volume developer

<u>Formula 2</u>
Rusk Deepshine Lightener 2-oz. SLB + 4-oz. 10-volume developer

Isolate a circular section in the crown area where hair splits naturally and secure. On remaining strands, create diagonal slice foil sections and apply Formula 1, working around the head. Apply Formula 2 to remaining strands and process 45 minutes.

174

Orange Squash

Christel Lundqvist
British Colour Technician of the Year
hob Salons
Great Britain

Existing Level: Pre-lightened
Target Level: 9-10 bright orange squash

<u>Formula</u>
Wella Color Touch Relights /34 + /74 + 1.9% developer

Process 30 minutes.

175

Bronze

Rodica Hristu
Goldwell International Platform Artist
Deberardinis Salon & Spa
Toronto, ON, Canada

Existing Level: Prelightened to 9-10
Target Shade: Rich bronze

<u>Formula</u>
Goldwell Elumen 1 part NA@2 + 5 parts GK@ALL.

Process 30 minutes.

176

Barely Pink

Patrick McIvor
Matrix Artistic Color Director
Patrick McIvor Color Studios
PA

Existing Level: Decolorized to pale yellow
End result: Very light pink

Formula
Matrix SoColor 1-oz. 11N + 10 inch SoRed RV + 20-volume SoLite Cream Developer.

Apply in foil sections to decolorized hair. Process 30 minutes.

177

Oyster

John Simpson
Goldwell North American Guest Artist
Lewis Salon
McDonald, PA

Existing Level: 9-10 prelightened
Target Result: A cool blonde with multiple reflections like mother of pearl. Neutralizes unwanted yellow tones.

Formula
Goldwell Elumen 60ml AB @ 9 + 3ml Pk @ ALL + 2 ml BB @ ALL.

Process until desired tone is achieved.

178

Color Melting

David Adams
RedCHOCOLATE
Minneapolis, MN

Natural Level: 5
Target Level: 4-12 in a gradual fade from dark to light

Formula 1
Aveda Full Spectrum 40g 4N + 4g Dark Yellow/Orange Pure Tone + 4g Dark Red/Orange Pure Tone with 40G 20-volume Color Catalyst

Formula 2
Aveda Full Spectrum 40g Dark Pure Base + 10g Dark Red/Orange Pure Tone + 2g Dark Yellow/Orange Pure tone + 40g 20-volume Color Catalyst

Formula 3
Aveda Enlightener + 10-volume developer

Formula 4
Aveda Full Spectrum 20g Light Pure Base + 20g 10N +8g Light Orange/Red Pure tone + 40g 20-volume Color Catalyst

Apply Formula 1 to roots, extending 3-4 inches from scalp. Next, “melt” Formula 2 from end of previous formula and pull through, stopping short of the ends. Apply Formula 3 to ends. Process 35 minutes and shampoo. Apply Formula 4 to the lightened ends. Process 10-15 minutes.

179

Violet Glow

Jonathan Gale
SoloArtists.com
Chris McMillan Salon
Beverly Hills, CA

Natural/Existing Level: 1-2
Target Result: Glowing streaks of vivid violet

Formula 1
L'Oreal Majimeche + 30-volume developer.

Formula 2
Matrix Prizms.Plus Vibrant Violet

Prelighten desired strands with Formula 1 until hair reaches a cream color. Apply Formula 2 to prelightened sections.

180 *Teal*

Rodica Hristu
Goldwell International Platform Artist
Deberardinis Salon & Spa
Toronto, ON, Canada

Existing Level: Prelightened to 9-10
Target Shade: Teal blue

Formula
Goldwell Elumen BB@ALL + GN@ALL + 1 drop NA@2 + Clear (optional).

Alternate Formula
BB@ALL + GN@ALL + 1-2 drops YY@ALL + 1-2 drops NA@2

181

Platinum Punk

Mia Liguori McHugh
Scruples International Haircolor Educator and
Vice President of Creative
Lakeville, MN

Natural Level: 5
Target Level: 3 with bright red pieces

<u>Formula 1</u>
Scruples Color Art 2-oz. 3P + 2-oz. Color Art Processing Solution

<u>Formula 2</u>
Scruples Power Blonde Lightening Powder + Pure Oxi 20-volume Crème Developer

<u>Formula 3</u>
Scruples Urban Shock Glaze 1-oz. Crazed Red with no developer

Apply Formula 2 to large, random foil slices. Apply Formula 1 to all remaining strands. Process 20 minutes, rinse and shampoo. Apply Formula 3 to all strands, process 30 minutes.

182 Bubble Gum Pink

Sue Pemberton
Joico Vero K-PAK International
Artistic Director
Las Vegas, NV

Existing Level: 9-10 prelightened
Target Level: 10 modern bubble gum pink

Formula
Joico Vero K-PAK Intensifiers ¾ Clear + ¼ Magenta with no developer.

Process 20 minutes or until desired shade is achieved.

183 Maya Blue

Silas Tsang
NAHA Color Finalist
Blushes Hair & Day Spa
Ottawa, ON, Canada

Natural/Existing Level: 7
Target Result: Vivid blue

Formula 1
L'Oreal Platinium Plus + 30-volume developer

Formula 2
L'Oreal Luocolor 1-inch 2.11 + ½ tube 10 + Luocolor 25-volume developer.

Prelighten desired strands with Formula 1. Apply Formula 2 to prelightened sections. Process 10 minutes.

184

Brandy

David Adams
RedCHOCOLATE
Minneapolis, MN

Natural Level: 6
Target Level: 6-10 rich, multi-tonal browns and reds

Formula 1
Aveda Full Spectrum 6Y/O + 10-volume Color Catalyst

Formula 2
Aveda Full Spectrum 8O/R + 30-volume Color Catalyst

Formula 3
Aveda Shades of Enlightenment Twilight + 30-volume Color Catalyst

Formula 4
Aveda Full Spectrum 10V/B + 30-volume Color Catalyst

Apply Formula 1 to new growth at the roots. Alternate Formula 2 and 3 in diagonal, sliced foil sections throughout the crown area. Apply Formula 4 to all remaining strands.

185

Screaming Red Highlights

Beth Minardi
BTC Color Education Director
Minardi Salon
New York, NY

Existing level: 3-4
Target result: Bright, fire-engine red highlights

<u>Formula</u>
Redken Shades EQ 1-oz. 06R + ½-oz. 08C + 1/2-oz. Red Kicker + SEQ Processing Solution.

Apply to prelightened (orange or gold) strands. Process with heat for 20 minutes.

who's inside?

Thanks to these world class colorists who reveal their favorite formulas

David Adams
Kaz Amor
René Antonio
Berry Bachen
Jason Backe
Adriana Balea
Victoria Benham
Nancy Braun
Nelson Chan
Ellie Coates
Scott Cole
Susan Roberts Cooper
Tracey Cunningham
Devin Dawson
Dhaniel Doud
Teri Dougherty
Lucie Doughty
Christopher and Sonya Dove
James Edick
Michael Elving
Lucus Etcitty
Francesco Fricioni
Jonathan Gale
Lisa Marie Garcia
Stuart Gavert
Deborah Gavin
Maria Guasta
Anita Gutierrez
Rodica Hritsu
Christopher John
Gina Khan
Nury Lopez
Christel Lundqvist
Naz Kupelian
Mia Liguori McHugh
Nury Lopez
Doug MacIntosh
Patrick McIvor
Beth Minardi
Kazumi Morton
Sue Pemberton
Marie Robinson
John Simpson
Brian and Sandra Smith
Kris Sorbie
David R. Stanko
Charles Baker Strahan
Robin Sween
Silas Tsang
Alexis Unno
Lisa Vann
Maryl Velbeck
Kim Vo
Joel Warren
Clark Wood
Linda Yodice

appendix

Manufacturer Color Index

Affinage: 39, 51, 104

Ardel: 120

Aveda: 9, 42, 47, 53, 67, 74, 99, 147, 152, 157

Clairol: 7, 33, 36, 46, 50, 64, 65, 102, 122, 124, 138, 144, 146

Farouk: 27, 117

Goldwell: 5, 6, 23, 48, 49, 52, 77, 89, 95, 107, 115, 123, 128, 144, 145, 150, 151, 154

Joico: 4, 5, 8, 48, 52, 54, 89, 90, 94, 156

Kemon: 32

Logics: 17, 63, 91, 117, 137

L'Oreal: 9, 15, 19, 36, 47, 55, 58, 65, 86, 96, 98, 111, 118, 120, 124, 132, 138, 139, 153, 156

Malibu 2000: 116

Manic Panic: 146

Matrix: 25, 28, 66, 95, 103, 122, 127, 151, 153

Nelson J. Detox Crystal: 116

Paul Mitchell: 8, 24, 35, 50, 60, 87, 105, 110, 119, 142

Phyto: 82

Redken: 6, 14, 18, 19, 20, 26, 33, 38, 49, 54, 61, 64, 67, 68, 69, 70, 75, 86, 88, 90, 92, 94, 96, 106, 114, 118, 121, 125, 127, 139, 140, 143, 158

Rusk: 10, 11, 59, 76, 79, 97, 109, 131, 149

Schwarzkopf: 4, 14, 46

Scruples: 29, 41, 80, 81, 100, 101, 129, 130, 136, 155

Sebastian: 21, 72

TIGI: 34, 37, 59, 78, 108

Wella: 7, 10, 11, 16, 21, 22, 30, 31, 40, 51, 53, 58, 62, 64, 65, 71, 72, 73, 87, 93, 97, 98, 99, 116, 119, 126, 141, 142, 148, 150